Exploring Change in English Language Teaching

Editors

Chris

Paul Doyle

Christine Goh

MACMILLAN
HEINEMANN
English Language Teaching

Macmillan Heinemann English Language Teaching, Oxford

A division of Macmillan Publishers Limited

Companies and representatives throughout the world

ISBN 0 435 24053 6

First published 1999

Designed by Mike Cryer, eMC Design, Bromham, Bedford

The publishers would like to thank Louise Elkins and Phoenix
Publishing Services for their editorial work.

Printed and bound in Great Britain by The Bath Press

1002180662

2003 2002 2001 2000 1999
10 9 8 7 6 5 4 3 2 1

104253

Contents

Introduction – Learning to change

Chris Kennedy

Perceptions of change

A volume on educational change and innovation written in the mid-nineties was entitled *Changing teachers, changing times* (Hargreaves 1994). We can use such a title as a useful entry point for this collection. The phrase can be read in a number of different ways. No doubt readers will find additional meanings to those I shall distinguish here. This ambiguity and the different readings behind the title are themselves an illustration of the nature of change. Change cannot be viewed from one viewpoint. We all view change differently and we act and interpret the acts of others in different ways. The reasons we favour or resist a change, implement or reject a change are many, and to assume that those faced with change will act in rational predictable ways omits important political considerations (see for example Doyle's article in this collection). There is therefore no one truth or theory about change, but rather different perceptions of the change and its effects. Such perceptions can be powerful and anyone responsible for implementing change (we call these individuals 'change agents' – Kennedy 1997) will have to take account of them, something we shall see throughout the collection.

Before we discuss these issues further, however, we shall need to say a little about the terms 'change' and 'innovation'. Some writers use the two terms interchangeably; others take pains to distinguish between them in various ways. The general distinction made is that 'change' is unplanned and occurs 'naturally', whereas 'innovation' is deliberate and planned, with goals and outcomes, and intended to bring about improvement. These definitions beg a number of questions and conceal the unpredictable and chaotic nature of the topic. It is not always that easy in practice to sort out those influences which are unplanned and those which are planned, nor those aspects that are 'natural' and those that are 'deliberate'. There is the additional stylistic difficulty with certain established terms such as 'change agent' as someone who manages 'innovation'. For these reasons, we have found it simpler to use the term 'change' in this collection as a superordinate term which includes definitions of 'innovation' within it. We will therefore normally use the term 'change', but will on occasion replace it with 'innovation' when we see the need to highlight the planned, deliberate nature of change; when we need to contrast it with accidental or minor change (see for example Sergeant's article in this collection); or where there may be stylistic reasons for its use.

Changing times

But let us return to the second part of Hargreaves' title – 'changing times'. I have selected two meanings of the phrase. A paraphrase of my first interpretation would be 'times change': this refers to the changes which appear superficially at least to be unplanned and unconscious, a 'natural' evolutionary feature of human society. These are the sorts of large-scale and long-term changes in society which are due to changing socio-economic and technological conditions, whose prediction is not easy and the study of which is now the province of professional futurologists. It is difficult to identify distinct causes and effects underlying these sorts of large-scale changes just as it is difficult to identify particular individuals who influence them, but they have considerable effect on the field of education and our sub-activity within it, ELT. Lack of resources, a shift from command to market economies, globalization of commerce, and the spread of computer technologies are but a few of these large-scale developments. We can see the resulting 'changing times' in education and ELT in the form, for example, of alternative ways of financing and managing universities and schools, new curricula and syllabuses and the methodologies and materials that result from them. Such changes tend to be Western-dominated, since many of them are triggered by developments in the West and in particular the USA, and raise charges of neo-colonialism and the over-influence of Western thinking on curricula and methods in non-Western countries (see D. Kennedy in this collection).

And what of the alternative meaning to 'changing times', in which the verb is now transitive and there is an expressed agent – ie 'someone is changing the times'? It is difficult when talking of large-scale societal or cultural changes to identify particular change agents, and to isolate one group or individual is simplistic when we are dealing with a complex series of networks. National leaders, politicians, economists, scientists, business people, pressure groups, individuals in the course of their daily working lives, all play a role, though it would be difficult to quantify and localize the influence each individual or group had and on whom.

However, when we look at the effects of large-scale changes on education and in particular curricula and syllabuses in ELT, and if we use case studies to investigate particular changes, we can begin to identify some of the change agents involved, those who are trying to 'change the times', though they may not have thought of themselves playing that sort of role. The case studies in this collection are all concerned with a particular innovation in ELT which has come about as a result of larger-scale societal changes, and each identifies a particular change agent who has been instrumental in implementing the innovation. The link between societal change and educational change is perhaps clearer at the level of curriculum and syllabus (see Section 1 of this collection), since the cause-effect relationships can be more easily demonstrated, but even those case studies in this collection dealing with classroom change (in particular Roberts and Pollari in Section 3) where the link is not as evident, show how the roles of teachers and students change as educational philosophy changes, the latter itself being influenced by changes in society which necessitate the education of independent learners and thinkers able to put their skills to practical use.

The case studies are of three kinds. The first kind (Section 1) is nationwide large-scale change which is attempting to implement a new ELT curriculum and syllabus together with new methodologies and materials in public sector schools and colleges (Goh in Malaysia; Carless in Hong Kong; D. Kennedy in China). Edwards' article, the last one in this section (on the implementation of a quality improvement programme in a UK college), describes an institutional policy resulting from national changes, and thus provides a link between Section 1 on national change and Section 2 on institutional change. The second kind of case study (Section 2) is that of change taking place within institutions. The case studies in this section take place in private or semi-private language schools with fee-paying students (Sergeant and Doyle in Singapore; Bracamonte in Chile; Pinar in Saudi Arabia) and deal with changes in ELT methods, materials and technology. The third type of change described (Section 3) takes place within institutions but moves to the level of the ultimate implementers, teachers and students. Both Roberts (in the UK) and Pollari (in Finland) describe their experiences of implementing a form of action research in the ELT classroom.

So the case studies take us from large-scale national change through institutional change to classroom change. What links the case studies together, apart of course from the underlying theme of change in ELT, are two aspects. First, they are all personal accounts by those who have been directly involved in change and who in most cases have been given the responsibility for implementing a particular innovation. They are teachers but most have had to take on additional and different roles in order to implement the changes they have been faced with. From being teachers, they have become facilitators, trainers, advisors, managers, or a combination of these roles. They have typically occupied positions at a middle level between higher level policy makers and the ultimate implementers, teachers. (Roberts and Pollari in Section 3 have dual roles, both influencing the teachers and being teachers themselves.) Many are faced with the task of interpreting policies formulated by those above them and of finding ways of explaining and implementing those policies in terms of achievable objectives in the classroom – often, as we shall see, no easy task. They can all be described as change agents and in this sense all play a part in 'changing times'. Most have had no training for the additional roles they were asked to take on and it is one of the objectives of this collection to help those placed in similar positions in the future. This is not to say that there is any one way of dealing with change since it is always closely tied to a local context, but from the various case studies, which detail the reasons for failure as well as success, we may be able to extract a number of principles which can usefully be applied to different situations.

Changing teachers

The change agents, as well as playing their part in 'changing times', are also 'changing teachers', and this brings us to the second common link between the articles. They are all concerned with the crucial role played by teachers in the change process, since teachers are the implementers of the changes described. Teachers are in this sense change agents themselves and we need now to explain the ambiguity of the phrase 'changing teachers'.

There are at least three readings of the phrase, all demonstrated in this collection. One reading is the meaning 'teachers who change something', and this is the meaning we would associate with teachers as change agents, teachers as implementers of change in the classroom, who perhaps decide to, or have to, change their methodology or a particular teaching strategy. A second meaning of the phrase 'changing teachers' is that as the teachers take on the role of change agents and change their behaviour in the classroom so they themselves change – they are teachers who have changed. In thinking and reflecting on the changes they will make or have made, their attitudes and beliefs change, they add to their experience and knowledge, and they develop as professionals. There is a real sense in which they have changed as teachers. This professional development is also clear in the personal accounts of the writers in this collection, who in most cases, as I mentioned above, have taken on new roles and responsibilities as change agents – they are 'changed teachers' themselves.

Our final reading of the phrase 'changing teachers' is the one we have met previously. The meaning is 'someone changes teachers', that is someone is given the responsibility for managing the change of others in some way. We have referred to this person as a change agent and given the writers of these case studies as examples. The job of the change agent is to manage the change. Part of their task may be to change the behaviour of those who are the implementers themselves (in many cases, as we have seen, the teachers). So underlying the phrase 'changing teachers' are at least two sets of actors – change agents whose job it is to act on teacher behaviour; and teachers themselves who may have their behaviour changed by others or may change their behaviour themselves, and in so doing develop, or change, as professionals, themselves becoming change agents as they change or modify the behaviour of their learners in the classroom.

I have now mentioned behavioural change several times. Three strategies are mentioned in the articles to encourage behavioural change – rational approaches (information-giving); coercive strategies (forcing someone to change); and cognitive strategies (enabling individuals to reflect on and evaluate what they are doing and engaging with attitudes and beliefs). Change is a two-way process and although change agents may well be a stimulus for change, there has to be a movement for change on the part of the implementer, the teacher, otherwise the change will fail. Changing teachers in this sense will only come about if there is a change in attitudes and beliefs on the part of the teacher (cognitive change) and if the circumstances surrounding the change are such that they do not lead to resistance.

A model of behavioural intention provided by Ajzen (1988) is useful to explain the complexity of change. He believes a person's intention to act in a certain way will be influenced by three factors – the attitude of the person towards the intended action, the influence of peer groups and of superiors, and the degree to which the individual believes he/she has control over the change. (D. Kennedy's article in this collection gives some illustrations of Ajzen's model at work.) It is important to realize that resistance to change may be well founded and that it is not just an automatic defence mechanism put up against change (though that may be the case).

To summarize, there is an interrelated system of teachers themselves changing as they change materials and methods. In changing something in their classrooms, they themselves change not only their behaviour but their attitudes and beliefs. Interacting with this system is the external change agent (those who have written these articles) whose job is not so much to change the teachers directly but to create the conditions in which they can implement the changes.

Learning to change

What becomes clear as we read the case studies in this collection is that all involved in change are part of a learning process. Pupils and students are presented with new ways of communicating in their classrooms; teachers practise new methods and teach new materials; and those whom we call change agents have to acquire new skills in managing change successfully and dealing with complex situations they may not have been faced with before. All are 'learners in change' and 'learning to change'. This collection of case studies has been produced to try to help these 'learners' understand the processes of change, so that when faced with change situations, they may be better able to deal with them.

I have written a short introduction to each section and to each case study as an aid to readers coming to the articles for the first time.

Chris Kennedy has worked in several countries as ELT trainer, ESP adviser, and project director. His main interests are innovation management and evaluation, and language policy. He is Series Editor of ELT Review, a past Chair of IATEFL, and the present Chair of ETAC, British Council. He is Director of the Centre for English Language Studies, University of Birmingham, UK, responsible for postgraduate programmes.

National change

In this section, we meet instances of large-scale changes in the curriculum which are implemented by teachers in classrooms throughout a national system. The change agents in this section have all been charged in some way with implementing the change as teacher trainers responsible for communicating to teachers the ideas behind the new curriculum and the consequent changes required in methods and materials.

There seems little alternative to a top-down approach when changing national systems of education if there is to be an attempt at some form of uniformity and standardization in teaching and assessment across schools (Kennedy 1996). Goh's experience is as a trainer helping to implement a new Malaysian ELT secondary curriculum. She demonstrates how difficult it can be, at least in the short term, to ensure that changes involving different approaches to teaching and learning are accepted and used in classrooms by practising teachers who have their own established teaching styles based on long-standing attitudes and beliefs. It may indeed be that new approaches only fully take root when recruits to teaching, for whom 'new' approaches are part of their pre-service training and who have not yet developed their own teaching routines, enter schools and put into practice the training they have received. However, it is clearly important to train the existing teaching force in new approaches and Goh's article shows the different strategies that were adopted.

The first attempt at training existing teachers was a 'cascade' strategy (Gilpin 1997; Kadepurkar 1997). Trainers (themselves teachers), after receiving a one-week training course on the new approaches, conducted one-week orientation courses for selected teachers. These teachers were then expected to return to their schools to conduct seminars and pass on what they had learned from the trainers to their colleagues. In theory this appears to be an effective and efficient strategy for change implementation but the strategy made certain assumptions about change which were not warranted in the conditions which Goh describes.

The strategy assumed that the theory and the resultant practice of a complex curriculum innovation could be communicated both in a short space of time and using simple techniques of information-providing seminars (an example of rational strategies – see Introduction) and that those teachers (now change agents themselves) whose task it was to communicate the changes to their peers in schools would have the skills, experience and status to do so successfully. A further assumption was that the schools had the flexibility to deal with absences of their teachers on the courses and with the in-house training seminars when they returned. None of these assumptions was warranted and an alternative approach of school-based training was adopted using individual training packages for the teachers. This strategy was more successful according to Goh, but it still underestimated both the change required in the methodological beliefs of the teachers and the practical constraints of the classroom situation, such as heavy workloads and class sizes, reminding us of Ajzen's model of change (see Introduction). The strategy also highlighted the need for an intermediary within the school between the principal and the teachers, and Goh suggests this role should ideally be filled by the head of department. Goh goes on to illustrate how she herself performed such a role and evaluates its success.

The clear point that emerges here (and throughout this collection) is the importance of a change agent at this intermediate level to be responsible for implementation of the change. Such a role, linking higher and lower implementation levels, has to be a formal one within the structure of the institution. Goh found that when she temporarily gave up her position as head of department, the meetings she had held with teachers to try to get them to work collaboratively ceased until her return. Individuals and their own commitment and energy inevitably play a significant role in innovation, but if a change is tied to an individual without institutional commitment and without the change becoming part of the institution's culture, then it is unlikely to be sustainable once the individual moves on. Goh's article is a useful introduction to the collection in that it raises most of the themes which we will meet again in the other articles.

One of those themes is the idea of a collaborative culture through which a change can operate (Kennedy and Kennedy, forthcoming). The perceived lack of a collaborative culture is one of the factors which Carless identifies as a constraint in ELT curriculum change in Hong Kong. The change in Hong Kong was, as in Goh's study in Malaysia, the introduction of a nationwide curriculum which attempted to move teachers away from a teacher-centred, product-based transmission approach towards one which emphasized the process of learning and the pupils' role in it. The teacher moves from being in control of learning to facilitating it and activating pupils' knowledge.

Carless describes the almost impossible task given to trainers in these situations when those above them, typically within curriculum development centres or ministries, underestimate three things – the time required for training of teachers if they are to implement the change rather than just assent to it; the type of training required if a shift in attitudes and beliefs is required (telling teachers about a change is not enough – a cognitive approach is required – see Introduction); and the difficulties of the conditions in which teachers work (Carless mentions noise and class sizes as two constraining factors).

D. Kennedy, writing of his experiences as a change agent in China, was also involved in teacher training, resulting from a new syllabus emphasizing a more learner-centred and process-based methodology and materials. D. Kennedy reinforces the points made by Goh and Carless but adds two further elements to the complexity of attempting change. One is the sensitivity to local cultural norms required by those from a different culture. D. Kennedy was careful to operate within the norms of what he describes as a collectivist culture where the group is valued above the individual, and to be sensitive to a work situation in which a role culture preserved a strict hierarchy of control flowing from top to bottom of the organization. D. Kennedy comments that the top-down power-coercive policies which he describes are not liked by the teachers. He points out that at the intermediate level we are concerned with here, the change agent, acting between higher level policy makers and the teachers, must take care to avoid replicating such top-down policies when dealing with teachers, but without antagonizing the policy makers.

The second element D. Kennedy adds is the application of Ajzen's work, which was mentioned in the introduction to this collection. D. Kennedy looks closely at the work of four teachers and, using Ajzen's model, explains why some teachers adopted a particular change, in this case pairwork, while others did not. To remind readers, Ajzen's model explains that teachers' intentions to change will be influenced by three elements: their (positive or negative) attitude towards the change itself, others' attitudes towards it (positive/negative), and the teachers' own belief in their ability to implement the innovation, including practical constraints. D. Kennedy shows how one teacher negatively evaluated all three elements of the model and therefore did not implement the innovation; how one teacher was worried about loss of control in the class and this overrode the positively evaluated elements; how a third teacher, with all three elements positive, successfully implemented the change; and how a fourth implemented the change but evaluated the consequent experience negatively (lack of control in the classroom) and so did not continue using it.

Looking at individuals and how they react is of great value and reflects much more the reality of change implementation. Teachers do not accept or reject a change as a group. Some of them will adopt the change; others will reject it; others will accept parts of it. Such reactions may well develop and alter as the result of trying out the change. But without looking closely at the teaching situation, it will be impossible to diagnose why teachers are reacting in the way they do. Without the diagnosis, change agents, in this case trainers responsible for implementation, will be unable to decide on an appropriate course of action.

The fourth article in Section 1 is somewhat different from the others but highlights a number of the issues we have discussed thus far and looks forward to Section 2. As a result of a national change in the status of UK further education colleges which would now be increasingly self-financed with funding more closely related to results, colleges had to change their working practices. Edwards' article deals with one such change in working practices, the introduction of a quality management system throughout the college. Successful implementation of the system would result in the gaining of accreditation which would in turn, according to the management, facilitate the gaining of future teaching contracts.

We have seen the importance of culture in the D. Kennedy article above in which he draws attention to cross-cultural change across national boundaries. However, it is important to remember that cultural differences of a seemingly smaller scale can play a significant role in change. In Edwards' case there was a professional teaching culture and a management culture which tended to see the innovation in different ways. The quality system which the management of the college intended to introduce was one designed for industry which the teaching staff doubted could be applied to educational contexts. The management saw the introduction of the system as a means of sustaining future teaching contracts; the teaching staff saw it as an imposition from management that interfered with their teaching and questioned their professionalism. They considered it a paper exercise that, by diverting time from teaching, would not improve quality and might well lower it.

The cultural and ideological clash resulted in management forcing through the changes. This widened the gap between the two parties, and led to a 'lip-service' effect with staff completing the bureaucratic tasks required but not necessarily changing their behaviour. Edwards shows how difficult it is to evaluate such a change since it depends on whose objectives, staff or management, you take as criteria. She also points out that there are some signs of acceptance of the reform from staff initially resistant to it, raising the question of whether coercion is necessary in the face of unpopular reforms and whether, once the change is in place, former resisters adapt to it. Such a strategy may well be necessary in some instances, particularly where opposition is political rather than based on a professional objection to the change. If such coercion can be avoided through negotiation, this is to be preferred. If a change is forced on reluctant teachers, the dangers are that at best it is accepted but not implemented, or at worst the resultant conflict leads to withdrawal of the innovation.

Key points

- There seems little alternative to top-down change when change is required to national systems.
- Top-down change will only succeed with professional change agents operating at intermediate levels between the policy makers and the classroom.
- Change takes time and training which in turn implies a commitment to the resources required.
- Successful implementation of change involves changing attitudes and beliefs as well as creating favourable working conditions for change, taking into account those people likely to influence implementers.
- National and organizational cultures and potential cross-cultural conflict need to be considered in any strategy for change.

Nationwide curriculum innovation: how do we manage?

Christine Goh

Introduction

Curriculum innovation at the national level is an ambitious endeavour. It requires massive planning efforts, substantial sums of money and extensive retraining of teachers. All this is necessary even before new syllabuses are implemented inside the classroom. How does curriculum innovation on such a scale take place, and who actually manages it? My article aims to explore this question by discussing a recent curriculum innovation in Malaysia. It describes the process involved and discusses key issues by examining the implementation of the English language syllabus in the new curriculum. A case study of a large secondary school is included.

Reasons for curriculum innovation

Nicholls (1983:4) defines an innovation as 'an idea, object or practice perceived as new by an individual or individuals, which is intended to bring about improvement in relation to desired objectives, which is fundamental in nature and which is planned and deliberate'. It was precisely the intention to bring about improvement in the education system in Malaysia that led the Cabinet Committee to review the objectives and effectiveness of the education system. It published its report in 1979, and a number of changes to the curriculum were proposed (Ministry of Education 1985).

On the recommendations of the Cabinet Committee, the Ministry of Education reviewed the entire national school curriculum. As a result, the Integrated Curriculum (*Kurikulum Bersepadu*), as it came to be known, was developed and introduced in schools. It began in 1982 with a piloting of the primary school curriculum, followed by a full introduction the year after. The secondary school curriculum was introduced in January 1988.

The innovation process

The Ministry of Education made extensive preparations for implementing the Integrated Curriculum, using seminars, the mass media, information leaflets and books to make people aware of the new curriculum. New syllabuses for all subject areas were

Our first case study takes us to Malaysia and a major national curriculum reform which affected the syllabus, materials and methodology of all school subjects. In this article, Goh looks at what happened when the new English curriculum was introduced. The Malaysia example is in many ways a typical top-down national reform, with policy being set at the highest levels of government and implemented through the various levels of administration from ministry to curriculum centre to schools and finally classrooms.

developed. Each syllabus contained the aims, the instructional objectives, and a list of contents. These general syllabuses were designed for use throughout the primary or secondary school years. In addition, a detailed description of the contents to be covered in each year was produced. These syllabus specifications constituted the minimum requirements for a particular academic level. Meanwhile, publishers were invited to produce new coursebooks written in line with the requirements of the new curriculum.

One key implementation strategy was the retraining of thousands of teachers. This enormous task was undertaken by the Curriculum Development Centre, which was involved in producing information and training materials, and conducting training courses. Teachers were instructed by the Ministry of Education to attend one-week courses. These centralized training courses ran for a number of years before they were replaced by school-based training workshops.

In this process, my first role was that of a change agent, introducing the innovations to hundreds of practising teachers each year and providing them with the knowledge and skills to teach the new English language syllabus. My other role was that of a department head, managing the curriculum innovation at the school level.

Model for innovation

The curriculum innovation process in Malaysia contained some typical features of the Research, Development and Diffusion/Dissemination (RD and D) model described by Havelock (1971). The defining feature of such a model is that innovation is introduced from centre (consisting of experts and government agencies) to periphery (the end users). The RD and D model implies that in-depth research and planning have been carried out by a central agency. Results and products are then disseminated to the users in the innovation. There is a clear division of roles and labour, where the researchers and developers are seen as active contributors to the innovation while the users are merely passive receivers (White 1988).

As Figure 1 shows, the process of innovation was a rational sequence of activities in which different groups of people were involved at each stage. The initial research and development was undertaken by government agencies and textbook publishers. They produced the final package of innovation documents, dissemination procedures, and training and teaching materials. This was then passed on to teacher trainers and eventually to teachers. This process of innovation had many inherent problems, but for a country that wanted a major curriculum renewal it was perhaps the fastest way to do it. The way the innovation was disseminated and adopted is described in detail in the next section, which focuses on the English language syllabus for secondary schools.

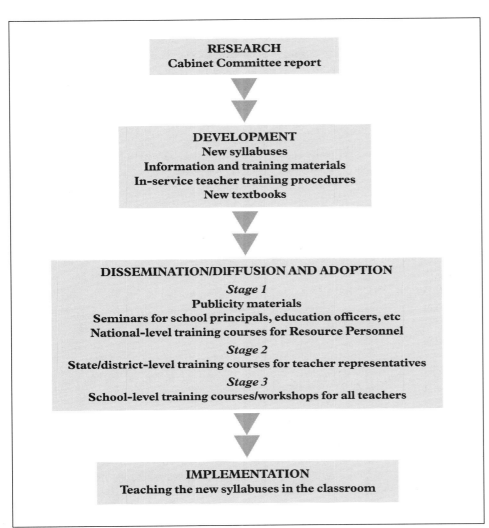

Figure 1: Innovation process of the integrated curriculum in Malaysia
(based partly on the RD and D model, Havelock 1971)

Implementing the new English language syllabus at the national level

The new English language syllabus was a radical departure from the old one, which concentrated on the teaching and learning of structural items in the first three years of secondary schooling and then focused on the development of communicative competence in the last two years. The new syllabus was planned as an integrated whole. It aimed to help learners acquire both linguistic and communicative competence simultaneously.

In practice, the syllabus had to be organized into learning units. For each unit, teachers had to choose a topic from a prescribed list and plan lessons that would integrate practice of listening, speaking, reading and writing skills. They also had to teach grammatical, phonological and vocabulary items in the context of the topic. All these elements were to be taught through a communicative approach, with an emphasis on student-centred learning activities. In addition, teachers had to make sure that moral values and literary elements were 'infused in an integrated manner' in each learning unit through suitable materials and activities (Ministry of Education 1990).

The new English syllabus required teachers to simultaneously handle knowledge (grammatical rules and language information), skills (listening, speaking, reading, writing), attitudes (moral values), literary appreciation, and communicative learning activities (pairwork, etc). This was clearly a complex undertaking compared with the old syllabus.

The first attempt: state-level courses

State education departments conducted numerous one-week courses to inform teachers of the changes to the English language syllabus and train them in the new approach. The retraining of teachers was staggered, beginning in 1987 for Form One [1] teachers and continuing in 1988 for Form Two and 1989 Form Three. Each set of teachers had to be trained a year ahead of the introduction of the new syllabus for their year. Training was provided by teams of Resource Personnel that consisted of education officers and specially selected senior teachers.

Resource Personnel were the first receivers of the innovation. Each year, before courses for teachers were held, about 50 national-level Resource Personnel attended a one-week course in the capital city, Kuala Lumpur. Organized by the Curriculum Development Centre, the course explained the instructional aims of the new curriculum and the political aspirations of the innovation. In addition, it provided Resource Personnel with considerable theoretical input that explained the rationale and the principles underlying the new approach in teaching. Resource Personnel also experienced new teaching techniques and training methods. To show that they had clearly understood the innovation, Resource Personnel had to plan sample lessons and carry out simulated teaching based on the new syllabus.

Apart from this, there were also discussions and dialogues between Resource Personnel and representatives from various bodies within the Ministry of Education, such as the Curriculum Development Centre and the Examination Board. Although these were opportunities for Resource Personnel to voice their concerns and doubts about the innovation, it was clear that their task was to disseminate important information about the new curriculum, not to change any part of it.

Back in their respective states, Resource Personnel ran one-week courses for teachers. These were loosely modelled after the one they had attended in Kuala Lumpur, but the contents were modified in order to cater directly to the needs of the teachers. The first part of the course dealt with the rationale for the curriculum innovation. This was done at plenaries and was usually followed by small group discussions. The rest of the course

---

[1] Students in Malaysian secondary schools are divided into 'forms'. Form One is the first year of secondary school, Form Two the second year, etc.

was directly related to the new English syllabus. Most teachers who attended the courses found the new syllabus interesting but were wary of the demands it would make on them. They knew, however, that it was impossible for them to reject it as the directive to teach it came from the government.

The dissemination and adoption process of the new syllabus was effected through two common innovation strategies. These are power-coercive and rational-empirical (Chin and Benne 1976:40). A power-coercive strategy seeks 'to mass political and economic power behind the change goals which strategists of change decided are desirable'. In the case of the innovation under discussion, there was no doubt as to whether teachers would adopt the new syllabus. It was presented to them not as a proposal, but as the product of careful research and planning, a better alternative to the existing syllabus. Most importantly, the new syllabus was legitimized through the power and authority of the Ministry of Education. The empirical-rational strategy, on the other hand, assumes that people are reasonable and will be open to rational explanation of the benefits of the innovation, especially if they stand to gain from it. In the training courses for teachers, for example, at least two days were spent on explaining different aspects of the new curriculum. When it came to the new English syllabus, the advantages of the new approach were constantly highlighted. Combined with input on the latest developments in language teaching, this appealed to many teachers. They felt that their professional image was being enhanced through the application of some of the latest teaching methods.

Weaknesses in the courses

In spite of the efficient way in which courses were organized throughout the country, feedback to the Ministry of Education suggested that these courses had not produced the desired results. Many teachers, for example, were still teaching in 'the old way'. Some of the inherent limitations of the existing innovation process also became painfully clear. After two years of running these courses, the Ministry began to make alternative plans that could overcome some of the problems.

1 Dilution of information

Information on the syllabus change passed through at least three groups of disseminators. It began with the Curriculum Development Centre training the Resource Personnel, who later passed the innovation on to teacher representatives. These teachers then had to conduct in-house sessions in their schools to inform other teachers who were not present at the one-week courses. As the information filtered down these layers it became diluted, distorted or got lost along the way.

2 Lack of ownership in schools

While the courses were useful in disseminating change to a large number of teachers from many schools, they did not instil a sense of involvement and accountability in the individual schools. Some teachers complained of unsupportive school principals, who seemed to have their own reservations about the new curriculum. In addition, teachers who were not selected for the courses often did not feel personally responsible for its implementation. Those who did not receive any form of retraining simply proceeded to teach the contents of the new syllabus without taking into consideration the new approach.

3 Ineffective change agents

Some Resource Personnel who were supposed to create an 'amplifier effect' were, unfortunately, ineffective in communicating the change to course participants. As they lacked good presentation skills, their sessions were disorganized and unconvincing. In addition, some fresh graduates were selected as change agents even though this clearly contravened the criteria laid down for the selection of Resource Personnel. These young trainers often lacked credibility in the eyes of teachers who had had far more experience in the classroom.

4 High costs

Large amounts were spent each year on retraining teachers. The running of state-level courses required considerable sums of money as food, transport and accommodation for course participants were paid for by the Ministry of Education. Other kinds of expenditure included training materials and remuneration for Resource Personnel.

5 Interruptions to lessons

Since most of these courses were conducted during termtime, lessons were cancelled for the entire week while the teachers were away. Sometimes the situation became quite critical when courses for different subjects were conducted concurrently in an attempt to meet certain deadlines. Parents often complained about the missed lessons and discipline in schools usually deteriorated at these times. Schools which had teachers serving as Resource Personnel suffered twice as much because these teachers would be away for several weeks a year, conducting courses in different parts of the state.

The second attempt: the Package System

In order to ensure that the curriculum innovation would eventually be implemented effectively in schools, the Ministry of Education introduced a new method of diffusion and adoption. This was called the Package System. A school-based training method, it made use of information and training materials produced and sent by the Curriculum Development Centre to every secondary school in the country. This method was used in retraining teachers for Form Four and Five classes.

The materials consisted of general topics like the national educational philosophy, the role of teachers in the new integrated curriculum, the school culture, and the inculcation of moral values. These topics were originally handled by state education officers in plenary sessions during the one-week courses. They were now to be delivered by school principals, their assistants and other senior teachers. There were also ample training materials for the new syllabus which comprised video cassettes, worksheets, and manuals for conducting training. The head of the English department became the facilitator for the training sessions.

With the implementation of the Package System, Resource Personnel no longer had to provide state-level training for teachers. Their role had changed to that of district-level consultants. They continued to attend centralized training and other courses to upgrade their knowledge and skills. As consultants, they visited schools at the request of school principals who needed advice on the new syllabus, and helped department heads conduct training sessions.

The Package System also made school principals directly responsible for managing the curriculum innovation in their schools. The authorities hoped that this would instil a greater sense of ownership and accountability at the school level. It was also, perhaps, a tacit acknowledgement that a more realistic and effective way of increasing uptake and managing the innovation would be from within the institutions affected by the change.

Advantages of the Package System

In comparison with the one-week courses, the Package System had several advantages:

1 Increased uptake

Previously, when teachers attended one-week courses, places were limited so only selected teachers from each school could attend. The Package System, however, enabled all English teachers to be involved at the same time. Since they received the same information through the same channel, the risk of dilution and distortion of information was greatly reduced.

2 School ownership and accountability

There was a notable increase in ownership and accountability at the school level. School principals and their assistants were directly affected by the new approach. Their professional reputation would be greatly enhanced if the in-house training sessions were properly conducted. On the other hand, if visits by officers from the Education Department showed that implementation had been slack, the result could be quite damaging. Schools therefore paid a great deal of attention to the planning of in-house courses.

3 Peer influence and collegiality

The facilitators for the in-house training sessions were heads of departments and other senior teachers. These were people the teachers were familiar with and who were often regarded as opinion leaders within their own departments. Their involvement as change agents could therefore influence the teachers to consider the change more favourably. Moreover, when teachers spent time together as a group working on a new training programme, it promoted collegiality. This is essential for successful curriculum innovation (White et al. 1991:167).

4 Minimal interruptions to lessons

With the abolition of state-level courses, there was no longer the problem of a great number of teachers being away at the same time. Training could now be conducted at those times that did not interfere with their normal teaching hours. Resource Personnel who were senior teachers did not have to miss their classes as often as they used to, since consultation with schools was carried out after school hours.

Setbacks in implementation

We have just looked at how curriculum innovators at the national level decentralized dissemination and adoption through school-based training and by making school principals personally responsible for the success of that training. This seemed an effective way of ensuring that teachers implemented the innovation. It would, however, be naive to assume that receiving training in teaching the new syllabus would naturally lead to adopting and implementing it. The proof of implementation is inside the classroom: the private domain of the language teacher only occasionally visited by subject inspectors and principals. Unless teachers begin to feel positive about a new way of teaching, all the good intentions of innovators will be wasted.

As one of the Resource Personnel I came into contact with hundreds of teachers, many of whom expressed concern about the new English syllabus. Since these teachers were the intended users of the curriculum innovation, their negative perceptions constituted severe setbacks to its implementation. These perceptions are discussed below.

1 Additional workload
Teachers saw the new syllabus as making new and added demands on them. Some saw the new teaching methods as an unnecessary burden that upset their well-established routines. Teachers were used to relying heavily on textbooks for every lesson, but with the new syllabus they were expected to prepare more of their own teaching materials, especially worksheets, which became the order of the day. They were also required to plan pair and groupwork. The new system of keeping lesson records was seen as tedious, and teachers with many years of experience found this particularly annoying. As well as facing new demands in teaching English, teachers, especially those who taught other subjects, experienced an overall increase in workload. Those who wanted to implement the new syllabus often found it difficult to spend extra time on developing more teaching materials and aids. With the additional workload, it also meant that many had little time to reflect on the benefits of the new curriculum.

2 Large class size
As it was normal to have classes of 40 or more students, teachers had difficulty carrying out groupwork and pairwork. Monitoring students' performance was a real problem since as many as ten groups could be involved at one time. Moreover, in classes where discipline was a problem, group activities were often abused by students. As a result, many teachers found themselves going back to a teacher-dominated, chalk-and-talk approach.

3 Lack of teaching ideas
Since the use of groupwork and pairwork was a relatively new approach, many teachers who were extremely effective in a teacher-centred way of teaching found that they soon ran out of ideas. This problem was often compounded by the fact that some teachers did not have a clear understanding of the underlying principles of the new approach. As a result, they were unable to develop and improvise learning activities once they had exhausted the 'bag of tricks' handed to them at training sessions.

4 Lack of personal involvement

Many teachers did not take a personal interest in the new syllabus as they felt they did not have any say at all in its formulation. They felt they were merely passive receivers whose role was not to question why, but simply to understand the blueprint and implement the syllabus in the classroom. They also felt they had no real bargaining power with regard to what to teach and how to teach it since everything had been prescribed to them.

Teachers' often negative perceptions about curriculum innovations such as those just mentioned are nothing new. In her discussion about managing innovations, Nicholls (1983) identified teachers' perceptions of changing practices and increased workload as a common problem associated with innovation. Cases of teachers' attitude have also been documented (see for example Young and Lee 1985). Everard and Morris (1985:171) have also warned innovators 'to address themselves not just to the world they see, but also to the world other people see, however misguided, perverse and distorted they may think the outlook of others to be'.

5 Weak follow-up

Teachers' negative perceptions were not the only setback in the implementation of curriculum innovation. Another problem was the fact that there was little follow-up or professional support given to the teachers after the training sessions. The one-week courses were useful in reaching the maximum number of teachers possible in a relatively short time. These were, however, one-off events and could not ensure that teachers had properly understood and acquired the necessary skills to adopt the new syllabus. This problem was partially addressed by the Package System which allowed teachers to review training materials as and when they wanted. But given the increased workload, some teachers probably never found the time to do this.

6 Ineffective monitoring

Another shortcoming of the implementation was that it was not always easy to establish whether teachers were actually teaching according to the new syllabus. Although many were observed by specialist inspectors, school principals, and, on some occasions, Resource Personnel, these observations were sporadic due to the large number of teachers involved. Some teachers were not observed at all. As a result, the answer to whether teachers were implementing the syllabus effectively was often inconclusive.

The success of any innovation should be judged by the end-users' willingness and ability to implement it. Its failure is the result of them having neither the will nor the skills to put it into practice. How then do we manage the implementation of a new curriculum so that it will have a chance of surviving? In the next section, I shall discuss some practical steps that I took when I was the head of the English department in a school. My aim then was to ensure that all the English teachers would at least try to implement the new syllabus.

Implementing the new English syllabus in school: a case study

To manage the implementation of the new syllabus, I set up a professional support system for the fifteen English teachers in my department. My goal was to help them develop the will and the skills I believed to be so necessary for carrying out the requirements of the new syllabus.

Objectives

Although my overall aim was to ensure the successful implementation of the new syllabus, my immediate concern was to help teachers to begin teaching it. I had several objectives. Firstly, I wanted to ensure that teachers who were convinced or partly convinced of the benefits of the new English syllabus got as much help as possible to teach it. Secondly, I hoped that teachers who were resistant to the syllabus would get a chance to discuss their reservations. I also wanted to win them over by providing them with opportunities to learn how other colleagues had successfully taught lessons based on the new syllabus. Thirdly, I wanted to create opportunities for teachers to reflect more on their teaching. Finally, I hoped to get feedback from teachers so that we could identify problems and consider appropriate solutions.

Strategies

I began by making use of regular departmental meetings. Apart from discussing administrative matters, I had teachers talk about their experiences when teaching the new syllabus. They were also asked to identify problems that they wanted to deal with. In one of the subsequent meetings, I suggested meeting at another time where we could show one another some teaching techniques that we had been using. The response from the teachers was enthusiastic as they were eager to get more ideas they could use in the classroom. They did, however, voice some reservations about the extra demands on their time. The school principal had made it clear that all departmental meetings would have to be on a Saturday so that lessons would not be disrupted. This meant teachers had to give up part of their weekends.

In-house workshops
The first workshop was called the ELD Get-together. I had deliberately chosen this name to give it a more friendly atmosphere. A few weeks before, teachers who volunteered to present their ideas told me the learning activities they wanted to share with the group, for example activities for teaching grammar, vocabulary and language skills. A programme was drawn up. Coffee and cakes were ordered – an essential part of the programme! The meeting was a success and I took the opportunity to encourage teachers to continue sharing their ideas by contributing to a resource bank.

Peer observations
In addition to the workshops, we also carried out peer observations of lessons. Teachers could invite any colleague to sit in during their lessons. This was different from the classroom observations done by the senior assistant, who was required by the Ministry

of Education to assess how far teachers had implemented the syllabus. The objective of peer observations was developmental. It aimed to give teachers an opportunity to reflect on their own teaching and discuss it with another colleague. The lessons that were observed provided an important context for this discussion. I gave everyone a set of guidelines as a framework for observation and discussion which they found useful.

The response to the peer observations was very positive. Teachers did not feel threatened by the presence of someone they had personally invited. A number of them said they had acquired new teaching ideas through observing others, while those observed said that they spent a lot of time thinking about their lessons. Teachers also talked to me informally about the lessons that they taught or observed, and in that way, I was able to obtain some useful feedback about the progress of the implementation.

Resource bank
While the in-house workshops and peer observations were successful, and everybody agreed that they should be conducted more often, the resource bank was less successful. Box-files were left at a convenient place for teachers to drop in their worksheets and other materials, but the response was poor. I reminded teachers several times, but other than materials deposited by a young teacher trainee and myself, the contents inside the box-files remained relatively unchanged. However, I continued with the idea of a resource bank by putting in a copy of each set of materials teachers used during the in-house workshops. Materials used in lessons during peer observations were also included.

A year after I established the support and feedback system described above, I went on study leave. Later, I learned that all the activities stopped.

A second go

When I resumed my responsibilities as the department head, I did not immediately revive the activities. It was coming to the end of the academic year and I also felt that it might be unwise to appear too eager to change the situation soon after my postgraduate studies overseas. Nevertheless, I started making plans for the new academic year. I began talking to some teachers informally to find out how they had been coping with the new syllabus. When they mentioned the problems they faced, I suggested that they bring these up for discussion at the next department meeting.

My intention of resuming the workshops was considerably helped by a memo from the school principal at the beginning of the new academic year. He directed all departments to hold at least seven meetings in a year. At the first English department meeting, we agreed that time would be better used for matters related to the actual teaching of English. Once again, the teachers were enthusiastic about the workshops. Four meetings were set apart for this purpose. We decided that three of these should be related to specific topics and guest speakers would be invited to take these sessions. The fourth meeting was planned as another show-and-tell session by teachers in our own department. My suggestion to call these four sessions 'Staff Development Programme' was promptly accepted. This new name was chosen to reflect the professional nature of the meetings and it gave 'respectability' to our new endeavour. The meetings were a success.

Figure 2 summarizes the different parts of the professional support and feedback system established in our department and their function.

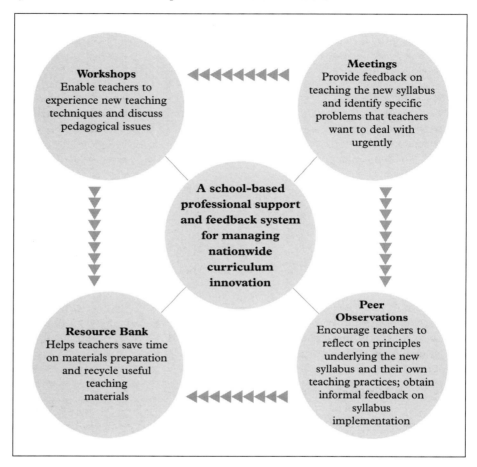

Figure 2: Components of a school-based professional support and feedback system for managing curriculum innovation at departmental level

Implications of the case study

Although it was a good decision to make the school principals responsible for the curriculum innovation in their own schools, the existing school administrative structure was not fully utilized. One group of people who can contribute greatly to the success of implementation are the heads of department. They have specialist knowledge of the subject, and they also keep in contact with subject teachers more closely and more often than principals and senior assistants (eg deputy heads) do. As the case study has shown, a department head can directly influence teachers to change their negative perceptions of the innovation by offering them practical professional support, such as increasing their repertoire of teaching techniques. This is helpful to teachers who not only have to adjust to new ways of teaching, but also contend with an overall increase in workload.

A professional support and feedback system is a useful way of encouraging language teachers to assess their own teaching practices. It can also raise their awareness about issues related to the new syllabus, and encourage them to share problems and seek solutions. Ideally, teachers themselves should request more professional support and avenues for feedback. Nevertheless, some top management decisions made with other aims in mind can also be exploited for this purpose. In the school situation related earlier, the memo from the principal was a case in point.

Encouraging teachers to think about their own values and improve their skills is a good example of a normative-re-educative strategy for innovation (Chin and Benne 1976), called a 'cognitive' strategy in the Introduction (see pvii). This strategy is based on the principle that people, being active and rational, must participate in their own re-education. Chin and Benne stressed the significance of a normative-re-educative strategy:

> These approaches center in the notion that people technology is just as necessary as thing technology in working out desirable changes in human affairs ... clarification and reconstruction of values is of pivotal importance in changing. By getting the values of various parts of the client system along with his own, openly into the arena of change and by working through value and conflicts responsibly, the change agent seeks to avoid manipulation and indoctrination of the client, in the morally reprehensible meanings of these terms. (1976:33)

For language teachers, 'clarification and reconstruction of values' involves a rethinking of their theory of teaching through discussions with others about what this theory is and what their concerns are. Without changes in teachers' attitudes, White (1988) noted, curriculum innovations will be superficial and short-lived. An important task for department heads, therefore, is to promote this change.

Apart from working with teachers, the head of department can also be a vital link between them and the school principal. Both teachers and management will benefit from this open channel of communication. Teachers can be assured that their problems will come to the attention of the school principal. This is crucial, as some teachers might be reluctant to put extra effort into an innovation because of what they perceive as a lack of support and recognition from the school management. From an administrative perspective, school principals and their assistants, who have the task of managing more than ten syllabuses, can receive valuable feedback on the actual implementation of the innovation. This comes directly from the teachers, as well as from the head of department who monitors the implementation informally through the system presented in Figure 2.

It is clear that the heads of department have an indispensable role in managing a new curriculum. However, like other teachers, they also have to shoulder a heavy teaching load. In addition, they have to see to daily administrative matters within the department. This may discourage them from taking upon themselves the task of managing the implementation of the new syllabus. As department head, I had two personal reasons for wanting to see the syllabus successfully implemented. Firstly, I believed that in spite of the additional workload the new English syllabus was placing on teachers, it was indeed a change for the better. If properly implemented, it could make learning English enjoyable and productive for students of all abilities. My second reason had to do with the fact that I was a member of the national-level Resource Personnel, entrusted with the task of disseminating the innovation. I felt that I would have failed in my responsibilities if the syllabus was poorly received and used by teachers in my own school, not to mention that it would also be deeply embarrassing for me. Therefore, I was prepared to spend a great deal of my time thinking and planning ways of helping the teachers and the principal of my school.

Heads of department who may not feel the same way as I did would probably need some external motivation for taking on the role of a manager of innovation. The relevant authorities could provide incentives to help them take on this role. In particular, the authorities should review existing school organization and officially endorse department heads as managers of the innovation. There are many ways this can be done, but a further discussion of these different ways is beyond the scope of this article.

Conclusions

For a centrally planned curriculum innovation to be accepted by teachers, it must be managed carefully at the school level. This calls for a strategy that directly addresses the various setbacks discussed earlier. In the case of the curriculum innovation in Malaysia, changing the dissemination method from state-level courses to school-based workshops actually had little impact on the day-to-day implementation of the curriculum. Besides developing a new curriculum, innovators need a comprehensive and realistic package for managing the implementation at the school level. The key managers here are not school principals, but, as I have argued, heads of department. These heads of department should be given all the support necessary to ensure that they do a good job.

Curriculum innovation on a national level is, indeed, an ambitious endeavour. Innovators must take steps to ensure that after investing so much time and money in disseminating the innovation, the final and most crucial stage – implementation – is not left to chance. Successful implementation lies in the hands of thousands of teachers in the country. At the end of the day, it is these teachers who will determine whether innovations that have been adopted through top-down measures will eventually be carried out inside the classroom. Nevertheless, with careful and effective management at the school level, the likelihood of a curriculum innovation surviving, even thriving, is extremely good.

Christine Goh taught English in Malaysia, and as National Resource Person, she trained secondary school teachers to implement the Malaysian national curriculum. Now a lecturer at the National Institute of Education, Nanyang Technological University, Singapore, she directs the Institute's EAP programme for international students and teachers on the MA in Applied Linguistics programme.

Large-scale curriculum change in Hong Kong

2

David R. Carless

Introduction

n this case study, I want to look at the management of change of an innovative cross-curricular initiative for Hong Kong primary schools, known as the Target-Oriented Curriculum (TOC). Under its previous name, Targets and Target-Related Assessment (TTRA)[1] the reform was intended to be introduced in 1993 but a number of implementation problems prompted a postponement. My own involvement in the TOC initiative has been as a teacher trainer for the subject of English; the perspective of this case study is therefore primarily from an English as a Second Language viewpoint, although some of the discussion arises more generally from the wider process of managing educational change. In the first part of the article I will describe the initiative and place it within the Hong Kong context. In the second part, I will focus on the management of change in this project, starting with the initial preparations for the change and then highlighting factors that made successful implementation problematic.

TOC framework

Origins

The Education Commission set up by the Hong Kong government in its report no. 4 (ECR4 1990) recommended that the quality of individual learning in Hong Kong schools would be improved by the development of a cross-curricular framework of targets and target-related assessment. The framework was intended to cover all subjects in the curriculum but initially would be developed to cover Chinese, English and mathematics through four Key Stages (KS) (see Figure 1 on p20).

Carless, by providing a similar example to Goh's case study, though this time at primary rather than secondary level, shows us the difficulties in large-scale curriculum change in Hong Kong and how the Education Department sought to solve problems that arose from the initial policy of curriculum change. Both case studies show how easy it is to underestimate difficulties in implementation at the level of the classroom and how time and training are important for success. The more complex the innovation and the more removed it is from teachers' existing practices, the greater the need to provide training and time for teachers if they are to adopt the change. One further important aspect of the change that Carless mentions is that of the linkage between the new curriculum and the testing of pupils.

[1] The name was changed in August 1993; for convenience I have used the term TOC throughout this article.

Key Stage 1	Primary 1–3
Key Stage 2	Primary 4–6
Key Stage 3	Secondary 1–3
Key Stage 4	Secondary 4–5

Figure 1: Year levels of Key Stages

A review of the Hong Kong school curriculum carried out for the Education Commission indicated a number of problem areas that needed to be addressed:

- an overcrowded and fragmented curriculum
- an overemphasis on the rote-learning of discrete chunks of information
- lack of awareness of the role of language in learning
- little allowance made for individual learner differences
- assessment methods focused primarily on ranking students in order

(Clark et al. 1994)

The TOC framework, designed to address these problems, was drawn up by the TOC Research and Development team in the Education Department's Institute of Language in Education (ILE). The team, led by four experienced expatriate curriculum developers, carried out research into similar curriculum reforms in a number of other countries (eg UK, Australia). They were supported by six Hong Kong teachers, and four teacher reference groups, each of approximately ten teachers, also provided feedback.

The product of their endeavours was a curriculum framework drawing on experience elsewhere and tailored to the needs of the Hong Kong school system.

Main elements

Given the complexity of the framework and to minimize authorial interpretation, I will draw heavily on published TOC documents to present the main elements of TOC. The TOC framework is an integrated system for improving the quality of teaching, learning and assessment in Hong Kong schools. It is a system for planning, designing, organizing, implementing, resourcing, monitoring, assessing and evaluating all aspects of teaching and learning (Education Department 1992a). The purpose of the TOC framework is:

- to allow targets to be formulated which express the purposes of education;
- to ensure comprehensiveness, coherence and continuity within the curriculum;
- to provide common concepts and procedures for curriculum design, curriculum development, implementation, evaluation and renewal.

The main elements in the framework are as follows:

- an integrated and progressive set of learning targets for the curriculum as a whole and for each subject at each Key Stage (see Figure 2)
- a progressive series of learning tasks by means of which learners work towards the learning targets
- a target-related assessment scheme for each Key Stage
- a means of recording and reporting individual learner progress in relation to targets

(Education Department 1992b)

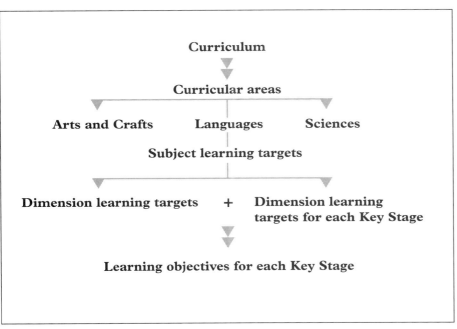

Figure 2: Hierarchy of learning targets

The TOC framework proposes a criterion-referenced assessment system designed to provide clear statements of student progress in relation to targets, giving credit for partial as well as full responses and recognizing strengths and weaknesses in the student's work. Target-related assessment aims to promote student learning through both ongoing formative assessment and summative assessment at the end of the year and/or Key Stage. The bands of performance describe what students can typically do at each Key Stage and how well they do it in relation to the targets (Education Department 1992a).

In summary, TOC provides a framework through which students work towards stated targets, through actively carrying out learning tasks, to be assessed by target-related assessment based on published bands of performance.

Hong Kong primary school context

Conditions in Hong Kong primary schools are not ideal and can have a negative influence on the process of teaching and learning. Because of Hong Kong's land shortage many schools are bi-sessional with a morning section running from about 7.30 to 12.30 and an afternoon section from about 1.00 to 6.00. Lack of space makes it difficult for pupils or teachers to store textbooks or teaching resources adequately. The location of many schools is undesirable: air pollution from industrial areas can be an irritant and noise pollution from construction sites, road traffic or aeroplanes is even more of a problem. In the Confucian tradition, diligent teachers and pupils strive to overcome these negative factors.

In the Hong Kong education system, primary school teaching is mainly a non-graduate profession with most teachers qualifying by means of a three-year pre-service teaching certificate, where they usually study a major and minor elective subject. However, owing to the demands of individual schools, practising teachers are often required to teach subjects for which they have not been trained. This phenomenon presents a particular problem for English, which tends to suffer from a shortage of subject-trained teachers. In addition, some teachers are recruited without having had any specialist educational training whatsoever.

In terms of teaching styles, Llewellyn (1982), Young and Lee (1987) and Morris (1988) indicate that Hong Kong teachers can generally be characterized as transmissive teachers. In other words, they tend to see their role mainly in terms of transmitting knowledge and information to the learner, with an emphasis on product and accuracy. Teachers often justify their transmissive teaching strategies with reference to 'covering the syllabus' and preparing for exams (Alderson and Wall 1993). More child-centred or discovery approaches (and TOC would fit into this category) are considered by teachers as inappropriate for exam-oriented purposes (Morris 1985). Pressure from parents and principals tends to reinforce this tendency.

Initial preparation for change

Piloting

Piloting was carried out in 20 schools between September 1992 and May 1993 with Primary 4 classes only, and since then a voluntary try-out scheme has been in operation. Evaluation has been carried out mainly through questionnaires to principals, teachers, pupils and parents in the pilot schools and via classroom observations by the Education Department Inspectorate and by District Education Officers. There was no attempt to carry out empirical research through the setting up of control groups to compare with the experimental classes.

The pilot scheme has been extensively criticized for being hastily set-up and for not offering sufficient support to the teachers in the pilot schools. In particular, the implementing teachers were only provided with three days' training and insufficient resources in terms of teaching materials. Furthermore the choice of pilot schools was mainly a result of the initiative of the principals or their Advisory Boards rather than the teachers themselves, so the decision was imposed on the teachers from above irrespective of their readiness or wishes. An additional weakness of the piloting was that the evaluation mechanism was not sufficiently rigorous.

Teacher support

The Education Department tried to prepare teachers for TOC implementation in a number of ways. Various documents were prepared for explanatory purposes, including a general introduction to TOC, learning targets and exemplar tasks, and programmes of study for each Key Stage (initially only the KS2 one was developed). A TOC Teacher Education team on secondment from the Institute of Language in Education (ILE) and Colleges of Education was set up to provide general and subject-specific teacher education in the form of three-day seminars and follow-up workshops. School teachers attended sessions with departmental colleagues and were able to work together in these school-based groups during workshop sessions.

Initial implementation schedule

A rolling implementation scheme was envisaged involving the commencement of TOC teaching firstly with Primary 4 only in May 1993. The decision to start towards the end of a school year was somewhat paradoxical but it was thought that this would allow a short trial period which could be reviewed before the next academic year. It was planned that more classes would adopt TOC in September 1993 and that through progressive implementation at both KS1 and KS2 by September 1994, the three core subjects of English, mathematics and Chinese would be taught entirely through TOC. In fact, as was mentioned earlier, the project was put on hold in April 1993 and the Director of Education appointed an Advisory Committee to review the innovation and plan a new timetable for implementation. It was then decided to implement TOC on an incremental basis starting with Primary 1 in 1995.

Postponement factors

In the next six sub-sections, I will review some of the key issues that made the management of change in this project problematic and so prompted the postponement.

In-service training

In-service teacher training is an essential part of preparation for the implementation of an innovative curriculum framework. Teachers need to acquire the skills and knowledge to implement something, particularly if it is highly different to their existing methods. Gross et al. (1971) highlight the problems of a lack of retraining, for if teachers are not equipped to deal with the implications of a new approach, they are likely to revert to the security of their previous behaviour and the desired change may not take place. Without sufficient retraining, even teachers initially enthusiastic about an innovation can become frustrated by problems in implementation and eventually turn against the project.

TOC training was carried out by the TOC Teacher Education section through a series of mass centralized three-day seminars for KS2 teachers from September 1992–April 1993 followed by half-day follow-up workshops (April 1993–December 1993). A revised two-day programme for KS1 teachers started in January 1994. Sessions contained a mixture of input and workshop-style task-based groupwork. The content comprised one general introductory lecture, including the reasons for change, and a series of subject-elective sessions covering topics like targets, tasks, schemes of work, TOC lesson planning, learner differences and assessment.

The reaction to these seminars was mixed and a substantial amount of opposition was expressed. Many teachers felt unprepared to begin teaching under TOC in May 1993 in Primary 4. The main complaints aired were a need for more extensive teacher training and the provision of more resources. The Director of Education acknowledged this:

> (TOC) is a very good concept and is widely supported. With hindsight we can say the implementation was a little hasty. We did not expect the amount of training to be insufficient from the school and teachers' point of view. (*South China Morning Post* 24/4/1993)

One of the briefs of the Advisory Committee on TOC implementation was therefore to review the provision of teacher training for the project. It was apparent that teachers required more assistance in understanding the TOC framework and preparing for its implementation. For the 1994–95 school year, the Advisory Committee therefore proposed that TOC teacher education should be school-based with a number of in-service days being set aside. There would be some input and assistance from TOC Teacher Education lecturers but there would also be periods where school colleagues would work together as a team. It was hoped that this would help to generate a greater feeling of ownership and commitment towards the scheme and enable teachers to adapt TOC to the specifics of their own school environment.

Practicality

Almost all innovations involve reinvention, ie 'the degree to which an innovation is changed or modified by a user in the process of its adoption and implementation' (Rogers 1983:175). Reinvention may be prompted by complexity, conflicting attitudes and beliefs or the practicalities of the classroom. The more complex an innovation is or is perceived to be, the less it will be seen to be practical. TOC has tended to be regarded by teachers as highly complex; a target-oriented task-based methodology represents a different terminology and approach that can easily seem threatening to teachers. Recent revisions to the framework and the learning targets for TOC have focused on simplifying concepts and making them more user-friendly and seem to have been well received by teachers.

A certain amount of reinvention may also be prompted by difficulties of catering for learner differences and organizing effective groupwork in classes that are often as large as 40. The president of the influential Professional Teachers' Union objected, 'we will not be able to promote TOC until there is a decrease in class sizes.' (*South China Morning Post* 24/4/1993)

As well as large class sizes, Hong Kong's high levels of noise pollution also put a strain on classroom interaction. The fact that many school teachers feel obliged to use a microphone, for example, may encourage a transmissive or teacher-centred approach, particularly when student utterances are often rendered inaudible by traffic, aircraft and construction noise. One of the factors in the reinvention of TOC is therefore likely to depend on the classroom realities of individual schools.

Resources

White et al. (1991) comment that an innovation which places heavy demands on schools in terms of time, personnel and money will be less likely to be taken up than one which has more realistic demands. This point seems highly relevant to TOC as insufficient resources were provided for schools to carry out the scheme within the initial implementation schedule. A sample programme of study for KS2 had been produced and the intention was for groups of teachers to use this as a guideline for their own schemes of work tailored to the needs of their students. The idea was praiseworthy in that by involving the teachers in the process of creating the syllabus, imposition from outside would be reduced. However, in practice teachers were not provided with additional non-contact time in which to rewrite schemes of work and furthermore they often lacked the confidence and the skills to do so.

Hong Kong primary teachers tend to be accustomed to placing great reliance on their textbooks; the thought of having to rewrite schemes of work, prepare additional teaching materials and integrate sections of their textbooks with tasks from their programmes of study was understandably a daunting one. The teachers' preferred option was the production of published materials, thereby easing some of their fears about workload and transforming the innovation from a conceptual to a more practical level. Bearing this in mind and with the obvious eye to commercial considerations, publishers have been producing their own TOC-style textbooks. Once provided with the more tangible and familiar tool of a textbook, teachers may find it easier to come to terms with TOC.

From the human resources aspect, there was also a lack of manpower mobilized by the Education Department for the TOC initiative. Programmes of study, task descriptions, exemplar tasks and details on assessment all needed to be developed but the drafting and fine-tuning process was delayed by the lack of personnel working on these areas. The TOC Teacher Education section has also tended to be short-staffed, putting a heavy burden on lecturers and so decreasing motivation to join the team.

Attitudes

It is widely acknowledged that the relative advantage of an innovation does not necessarily lead to its successful adoption. Rational–empirical strategies (Chin and Benne 1976) do not necessarily cater for the difficulty of changing people's attitudes and beliefs. Research by Young and Lee (1987), related to a 90-hour in-service course with Hong Kong secondary teachers, illustrates that attitudes are often firmly entrenched amongst the teaching profession. The course aimed to effect a more communicative orientation to the teaching of English but the results were disappointing in that little attitude change was discernible. They concluded:

> ... teachers' attitudes are a product of values and attitudes within a particular culture, and thus, of all the factors in curriculum innovation, they are the least susceptible to change. (Young and Lee 1987:84)

The fact that TOC implementation seems to require a considerable change in beliefs along the transmission–interpretation continuum may be a significant stumbling block for the scheme. On a more optimistic note, a more recent survey of attitude change in ELT in Hong Kong (including TOC) over a full-time 16-week in-service course showed a significantly more positive attitude towards TOC at the end of the course (Carless and Lee 1994). Whether similar results can be replicated on the kind of short-term courses required for TOC teacher training is a moot point.

Relationship between change agents and receivers

Education in the Hong Kong environment tends to be marked by a highly centralized strategy of curriculum policy-making and very limited participation in decision-making (Morris 1988). Llewellyn (1982) and Morris (1990) criticize the lack of co-operation between the Education Department and schools, illustrative of a lack of mutual trust.

A later survey reported in Hirvela and Law (1991:26) confirmed this view through the response to the following statement: 'The decision-makers in Hong Kong's educational system do not take into account the feelings of teachers when making language policy decisions.' Seventy-two percent of school teachers in the survey agreed with the statement and only 4 percent disagreed.

With regard to the TOC proposals, the relationship between the change agents (the Education Department) and the receivers (the teachers) does not seem to have been particularly harmonious and it seems likely that this background of mistrust may have been a contributing factor. In a forum organized by the political group Meeting Point to discuss the TOC project, the Education Department was urged 'to be more transparent in its decision-making process.' (*Hong Kong Standard* 25/4/1993). The Education Department seems to be perceived as a bureaucratic institution adopting a predominantly top-down approach.

In such a centralized educational structure there may be a tendency for teachers to *accept* an innovation without necessarily *implementing* it (White et al. 1991). Morris (1988) has already identified this scenario in his analysis of the introduction of a new economics syllabus in Hong Kong. He noted that teachers were willing to accept the rhetoric of the innovation but did not translate this into classroom practice. By linking the teaching and learning approach with assessment, the TOC proposals hope to avoid this outcome. Given the exam-oriented beliefs prevalent in Hong Kong, the focus on assessment in TOC seems to be well-conceived. A proposed change in methodology without a corresponding change in assessment may be ineffective but by linking methodology and assessment the TOC proposals have created the conditions for positive washback. As Morris suggests in an earlier paper, 'examinations must be used to promote curriculum reform' (Morris 1985:15).

Ownership

Although there has been teacher participation in TOC working groups, the teaching force do not seem to feel that the innovation belongs to them. This issue of ownership is an important one and MacDonald (1991:3) invokes a cautionary note: 'Teachers are, on the whole, poor implementers of other people's ideas.' However, in Hong Kong schools there is little culture or precedent for bottom-up change and furthermore there is a question as to how practically a bottom-up approach can be applied to such a large-scale curriculum initiative. Kennedy (1988) points out that in a centralized administration it is not easy for ownership to move down the hierarchy to the teachers themselves. Clark, the project leader for the TOC framework, has some particularly relevant comments to make on the bottom-up–top-down continuum:

> In the real world of today, an unrestricted version of 'bottom-up' curriculum renewal is not going to be accepted by governments, however much educationalists may propound its virtues. We are, whether we like it or not, in an age in which an element of 'top-downedness' is inevitable. Rather than resisting this, it seems more sensible for educationalists to attempt to guide their political masters into forms of top-down intervention that provide a broad sense of direction, but that empower and enable teachers to work towards the renewal of their own classroom action in ways that give them a sense of ownership over their own curriculum. (Clark 1988:447)

TOC curriculum renewal reflects the thrust of Clark's comments above but begs a number of questions. If the overall framework is imposed from above how genuine is teachers' ownership? To what extent do good teachers in Hong Kong also possess the skills to make them good materials writers or good teacher educators? Can teachers with little or no training in the subject which they are teaching contribute effectively to curriculum renewal at the classroom level?

Summary

I would like to summarize the main strengths and weaknesses of the TOC proposals. As I see it, the strengths are:

- TOC has been carefully planned in terms of the development of the curriculum framework.
- TOC is based on research into learning and the curriculum and on experience in Hong Kong and elsewhere.
- There is a high degree of experience and expertise involved in the project.
- The implementation schedule for TOC envisages an incremental approach.
- There has been some attempt at teacher involvement in an attempt to avoid the pitfalls of an exclusively top-down approach.
- By agreeing to postponement and review the Education Department has demonstrated flexibility and willingness to listen to feedback.

The weaknesses are:

- The initial implementation time-frame was unrealistic, eg insufficient time was allowed for in-service training and the provision of resources.

- TOC has been perceived as being unduly complex and difficult to interpret.
- Planning for implementation and how to overcome constraints does not seem to have been adequately addressed.
- The difficulty of changing attitudes and beliefs seems to have been underestimated.
- The relationship between change agents and receivers does not seem to have been based on mutual trust.
- TOC is perceived as being top-down, and efforts to create a general feeling of ownership have been largely unsuccessful.
- A rigorous evaluation mechanism was not put in place at the outset of the project.

Wider implications

I would like to conclude with some thoughts on the wider implications that arise directly or indirectly from the experience of trying to introduce TOC in Hong Kong.

- Teacher training is obviously a key issue; trainers need to be sensitive as well as experienced and knowledgeable. Teachers need to be reassured that what they are currently doing is still worthwhile and that the new approach is intended to build on and improve existing practice. Successful innovation in schools depends on the support and goodwill of teachers, or as Elliott (1991:54) puts it, 'There can be no curriculum development without teacher development.' Teacher training, therefore, should be ongoing and developmental rather than of an isolated one-off nature.
- It is desirable to improve the present conditions in schools before introducing innovations, eg more money injected into schools, better pupil-teacher ratios, improved pay, conditions and training for teachers. Fullan (1991) believes that effective educational change does not occur without improvements to the teacher's working life.
- Adequate manpower and resources, from both the change agent and implementer perspective, are a necessity for successful curriculum renewal. There needs to be good co-ordination, communication and mutual trust between these groups and other parties involved in the innovation process.
- A curriculum designed principally by expatriates must take into account the realities of the local classroom context and needs to be perceived as doing this by implementing teachers, otherwise 'tissue rejection' (Holliday 1992) may occur. Whenever possible, it is desirable that local classroom practitioners play a leading role in the innovation process. The design of a culturally appropriate curriculum may be more effective than importing an overseas model and seeking to change entrenched cultural and societal attitudes (Young and Lee 1987).
- The difficulties in introducing large-scale curriculum change cannot be underestimated. It is advisable to anticipate problems (eg resistance to change, lack of resources) in advance and formulate some strategies for how to tackle them. A gradual approach to change is likely to prove more feasible than a more ambitious one.

David R. Carless is a lecturer at the Hong Kong Institute of Education working in pre-service and in-service teacher training. He is conducting classroom-based research into the implementation of Hong Kong's Target-Oriented Curriculum.

The foreign trainer as change agent and implications for teacher education programmes in China

3

David Kennedy

Introduction

This article is based on my experience of working in a teacher education programme in China. The first section gives a background to the programme and to teacher training in China. This is followed by an introduction to the role of the foreign trainer in teacher education programmes in Chinese teacher training colleges and a discussion of how he/she might facilitate change.

The change

In the early 1990s a new syllabus for the teaching of English in Chinese middle schools came into effect. This new syllabus prompted the production of new teaching materials, and Jilin Province, where I worked, selected the most popular set of materials, *Junior English for China* (*JEFC*). This consisted of a set of four textbooks with cassettes, flashcards and posters produced jointly by the People's Education Press (PEP) and the publisher Longman with the aid of a grant from UNESCO.

It is claimed that the new materials foster a more communicative approach, with student-centred learning, an emphasis on oral and aural skills, and language presented for use, not study. The materials do retain more traditional approaches such as teacher control, memorization and drilling, and an emphasis on phonetics. However, the materials are a departure from the old, with the teachers encouraged to present new language in the target language, to help learners practise language in pairs and groups, to teach spoken forms before written forms, and to encourage a more cognitive approach in freer production stages where learners produce their own language rather than copy from texts or repeat after the teacher. The texts introduce dialogue and they are not intended for translation. Visual aids such as flashcards and posters and use of the tape recorder are incorporated into the materials, and the teacher's book gives detailed guidance for each lesson in order to assist with the change.

The materials aim to improve English language teaching with an intended departure from behaviourist theories of imitation, from rote learning and from grammar translation techniques. In reality they still allow for such procedures, with practice material expecting trainees to conform to dialogue models, and with drilling retained,

This case study from China reinforces the previous case studies in Section 1 and also looks at a number of issues centring round the social context of change. One issue is the sensitivity required by a change agent to local culture especially if he/she is a stranger to that culture. Another issue in this case study is the importance of the teaching context in change, particularly the training available and the conditions in which teachers operate once they enter the profession. Each of the two previous case studies have mentioned behavioural change and D. Kennedy here looks at specific examples to see how four trainees reacted to the same change (in this case, the introduction of pairwork). Kennedy's case study is valuable in the way it takes a national change and looks at how it is implemented with individual teachers at classroom level.

albeit in its new 'communicative' form. The materials aim to make lessons more interesting and vivid with the use of new methodologies and visual approaches to language presentation and practice. The textbook follows a five-step method: revision, presentation, drilling, practice and consolidation.

Teaching and teacher training in China

It is the teachers who have to implement the change; teachers who have had no say in the decision-making process behind the change in syllabus and materials; teachers who often feel alienated from the change and feel resentment at the top-down, coercive approach to its introduction. In addition, the low status of teachers, their poor working conditions and their low salaries result in a depressed profession with poor motivation. Change has brought the teachers extra work with more planning and the challenge of new materials and methods. With no increase in pay and no improvement in conditions, motivation weakens. Teachers often see no benefits in using the new materials and methods, and to them the costs are high as they suffer loss of free time and experience feelings of insecurity. Those teachers who are motivated to implement the change often become disheartened when obstacles block their way, obstacles which result from lack of professional support and training. Lin (1993:53) summarizes these points when he states that 'reform efforts have set high and diverse expectations for teachers by requiring them to learn more about their subject areas, to use texts that are becoming more and more difficult, and to use new methods in teaching. Yet, lack of motivation and lack of help result in very little change in the classroom. Accordingly, the traditional way of teaching dominates.'

Often, especially in rural areas, teachers who have to implement the change have no qualifications in English. Although after the late seventies the Ministry of Education aimed to improve training for teachers, Lin notes that despite these efforts 'only a few teachers have received training due to the lack of openings in teacher training schools' (ibid). Teachers implementing the change are in need of in-service training and although this is becoming available in some provinces, training is not always sufficient to meet the requirements of the teachers.

Trainees in teacher training colleges are also aware of the low status of teachers and some lack motivation before entering the profession. Cleverley (1985:12) points out that 'along with agriculture (teacher education) is the least attractive form of tertiary education'. Many trainees hope to build up strong enough connections to change their occupation before they are assigned to schools as teachers after graduation.

Just as low motivation is common to trainees and teachers alike, so is inadequate training. Cleverley goes on to note that teacher training courses 'are heavily oriented to teaching trainees the subject matter they must transmit in class ... less than a fifth of the time goes on teaching method, psychology and pedagogy ... time spent on practice teaching is minimal, four weeks in a four year course' (ibid:15).

At the teacher training college where I worked, trainees studied on a two-year course and language-teaching methodology was not introduced until the second year. The methodology course consisted of one lesson per week for one semester leading up to a three-week teaching practice in a local school. In the case of my own trainees it was not uncommon for them to have only three opportunities to teach a class. The rest of the time was for preparation and observation. At the college more emphasis was placed on improving the trainees' level of vocabulary, grammar, reading and translation skills than on teacher training. The course did little to prepare the trainees for the introduction of the new materials and methods. Even though the college was in possession of 30 copies of *JEFC*, nothing was being done by the English department to introduce these materials to the trainees one year before the materials were due to be introduced in schools.

The foreign trainer as agent of change

The foreign trainer must be aware of at least two important features when involved in the implementation of change in a teacher education programme: cultural differences and strategies of change.

Cultural differences

Foreign trainers may find two levels of conflict: a mismatch between their own national culture and that of the context in which they teach (Hofstede 1991) and a mismatch of management culture (Handy 1991). They need to be sensitive to both the national and organizational cultures in which they work. Foreign trainers who come from a national or organizational culture which recognizes the identity and voice of the individual must take care not to threaten the balance of management roles in a cultural context where individual personality is subordinate to a set of duties, rules and procedures which give stability and predictability to the organization. Instead, foreign trainers must be prepared to negotiate their own role within the culture for the successful management of change.

My experience at my teacher training college provides an example. With thirty copies of Book One of *JEFC*, and seeing the need for trainees to be introduced to the new materials and methods, I wanted to be involved in a programme to help prepare the trainees for their future teaching experience. Discussion with the department heads allowed me to gauge how far I might be involved, and with some compromises, the timetable was changed to incorporate one session of 110 minutes each week for *JEFC*. The session was not to have 'methodology' in the title and I had to be careful not to step on the toes of the methodology teacher and threaten her role. I was able, in addition, to observe the trainees on teaching practice, but again I had to be careful not to compromise the role of the class teacher and college observer by giving contradictory feedback.

The materials and methods I used in my sessions are largely the result of Western influence on ELT. They are a transfer from Western educational theory and practice. If such ideas are presented by trainers from outside China, care must be taken to ensure that Western value judgements do not become a feature of the teacher education programme. Teachers and trainees who feel that an 'alien' approach is being thrust upon them as superior to their traditional approach may soon feel resentment to the change and develop hostility to its implementation.

Strategies of change

I have already pointed out that teachers, having been subjected to a top-down coercive strategy (see Introduction pvii for the three strategies of change) may feel alienated from the change. This lack of participation in the decision-making process may cause resistance with the extra work it brings. Foreign trainers must be aware of this top-down strategy and the problems it carries, and in planning their own teacher training programme must avoid duplicating the approach. The foreign trainer must aim to balance the coercive strategy for change by adopting what was called in the Introduction a cognitive strategy, similar to Goh's 'normative-re-educative strategy' (see p17). This is a collaborative, problem-solving approach which aims to raise awareness of the change and involves those affected in making decisions about the degree and manner of change they themselves wish to accept.

Change threatens the values, attitudes and beliefs of those involved and teachers and trainees may feel that their beliefs, deep-rooted in their culture, are being challenged and questioned. For successful change the foreign trainer must plan a teacher training programme which eases this threat by attempting to raise an awareness of both the beliefs and attitudes of the trainees and of the principles behind the change. Kennedy and Kennedy (1996:351) note that 'if they are to be successful, (teacher training programmes) involve a change in teacher and student behaviour in the classroom'. With reference to the work of Ajzen (1988) on a theory of planned behaviour, they look at the relationship between beliefs, attitudes and actions, and examine reasons for teachers' failure to implement change in their behaviour in the classroom. Figure 1 will help to explain the relationship:

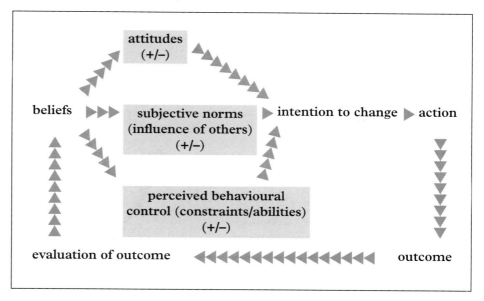

Figure 1: A model of change

Figure 1 illustrates that willingness to implement a change or aspects of a change derive from three factors: the individual's own belief about the action or behaviour (attitudes); the degree of influence on the teacher of others in the teaching situation (subjective norms); and the amount of control the individual feels he/she has over the change (perceived behavioural control). Subjective norms 'reflect not the individual's personal beliefs but what the individual believes others think about the behaviour concerned' (ibid:355). Perceived behavioural control consists of 'enhancing or limiting factors associated with the context' (ibid:356). The three elements interact to produce an intention to change and consequent action on the part of the teacher. The result or outcome of this action is then evaluated by the teacher and the evaluation fed back into the teacher's belief systems. The result may be that the teacher continues with the change, or decides not to repeat it. The following examples clarify the interaction of the three factors and show how four trainees varied in their approach to the implementation of pairwork (one aspect of *JEFC*) in class.

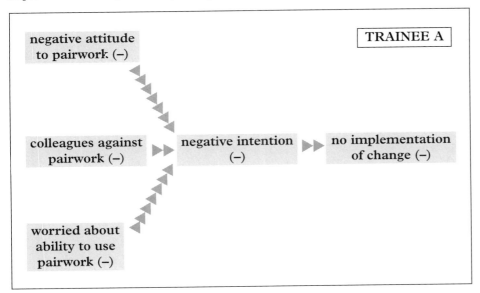

Figure 2: Implementation of pairwork (Trainee A)

Trainee A is unwilling to use pairwork in class due to his negative attitude. He does not believe that pairwork will improve the communicative level of his students. In addition, his colleagues are against pairwork, and he doubts his ability and skill to implement pairwork in the classroom. All three factors (attitudes, subjective norms, and perceived behavioural control) are negative. Not surprisingly, then, pairwork is not used and no change is implemented.

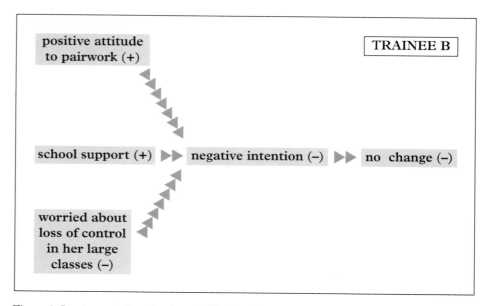

Figure 3: Implementation of pairwork (Trainee B)

Trainee B is willing to use pairwork in class and has a positive attitude with the belief that it will improve the communicative level of her students. The school supports the change but unfortunately she does not use pairwork as she is worried about losing control of her large class, especially in a culture which has high regard for student discipline. She believes pairwork is useful for small classes but not with her large class. The two positive factors (her own belief and institutional support) are overridden by the negative factor (a perceived problem of control). No change is implemented.

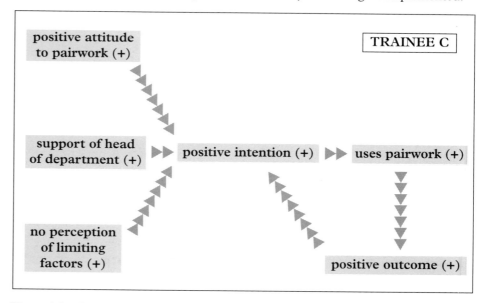

Figure 4: Implementation of pairwork (Trainee C)

Trainee C is willing to use pairwork and has a positive attitude, has support from his head of department, and sees no limiting factors at all. He believes pairwork will improve the communicative level of his class and uses pairwork. His belief is supported by a positive evaluation of the outcome and he believes that the communicative level of his students does improve. His optimism is maintained and there is change.

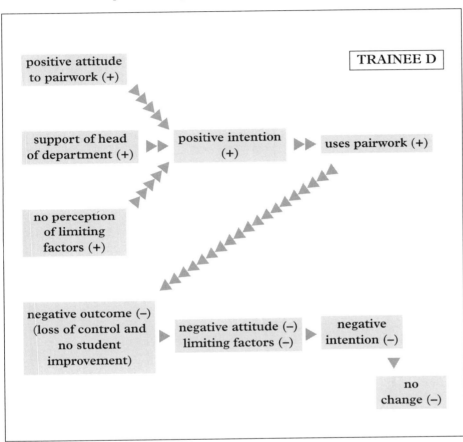

Figure 5: Implementation of pairwork (Trainee D)

Trainee D also believes that pairwork will improve the communicative level of her students. She has a positive attitude as a result, and with the support of her head of department uses pairwork in class. She sees no limiting factors. Unfortunately her optimism is misplaced, as she finds that the communicative level of her students does not improve. She finds that the noise level in her large class leads to discipline problems, a limiting factor she had not accounted for, and which is largely due to her inexperience of managing such an activity. The outcome is therefore evaluated negatively and she alters her belief, develops a negative attitude, and shows unwillingness to implement the change in the future.

Of course these are only four brief examples, and many combinations may be found among a group of trainees or teachers. In the last example the trainee evaluates the outcome negatively while another trainee in the same situation may have remained optimistic and tried pairwork again, but with improved classroom management strategies. Indeed, it is this type of evaluation process trainers should be encouraging on a teacher training programme.

Trainers must be aware of all the three factors (attitudes, subjective norms and perceived behavioural control) and their interrelationship in order to encourage change. Unwillingness to adopt change is related to attitudes, and as I noted earlier, to get trainees to change their attitudes and intentions requires awareness raising of beliefs. Subjective norms must also be dealt with by getting support from management, other teachers and trainees, and behavioural control by developing strategies to overcome the perceived limiting factors and to emphasize positive factors.

Trainees must be encouraged to try the change and evaluate the outcome. In evaluation they should be persuaded not simply to reject the change, but to think of the factors which led to its failure and to try again in the light of the evaluation, and see if the negative factors can be changed to positive. This way the trainees feel that they are involved in the change, with a professional evaluation process giving them a chance to participate, and giving them a rationale by which they can accept or reject aspects of the change. This approach may lessen the feeling of resentment of the coercive approach and give the trainees a sense of empowerment.

Suggestions for a teacher training programme

From the points made so far it is possible to list the following conclusions which are relevant to a foreign trainer running a teacher education programme to introduce *JEFC* in a Chinese teacher training college, and also to those working in similar contexts.

- The new materials are a departure from the old, requiring teachers and trainees to develop new skills and classroom techniques related to the new methodology.
- A top-down, coercive strategy for implementing the change may cause resentment amongst teachers and trainees.
- There is lack of motivation for teachers and trainees to implement the change due to the problems of the low status of teaching as a profession, lack of adequate training, poor resources and low pay.
- Foreign trainers need a culturally sensitive approach to the management of the change and must take care not to threaten the management culture of the organization/institution.
- Foreign influence on the materials and methods may cause resentment amongst teachers and trainees.
- A cognitive approach to the management of change may balance the coercive approach (see Introduction pvii for strategies of change).
- Raising awareness of attitudes and beliefs amongst teachers and trainees is an important factor in a cognitive approach in order to change their behaviour in the classroom.

- Gaining support of others in the management structure is an important factor for aiding the change process.
- Overcoming perceived limiting factors to the change (such as class size or lack of skills) will assist teachers and trainees to implement the change.
- Evaluation of new materials and methods by teachers and trainees is vital to give them a firm base from which to accept or reject aspects of the change. Evaluation is a tool which helps the teachers and trainees to make informed decisions and participate in the change process.

Trainees need to be introduced to new skills and classroom techniques related to the new methodology (such as drills, pairwork, substitution tables, presentation of new language and using the tape recorder). A collaborative, problem-solving approach ensuring trainee-centred learning will help to counteract the coercive strategy already in action and will attempt to increase trainee motivation through participation. The methodology in new materials must be presented in a way which stimulates the trainees' cognitive abilities and helps them to relate the principles behind the methodology to their own beliefs, attitudes and experience. The use of trainee diaries, loop input and action research are possible methods which can achieve these aims. Raising trainees' awareness of their own attitudes and beliefs is important for relating these to the principles of the methodology. Involving trainees in evaluation procedures and encouraging them to initiate their own evaluation procedures is a necessary component of a teacher training programme. It is vital that foreign trainers should help trainees to overcome limiting factors to the change and emphasize the importance of support of others in the management structure. Evaluation procedures can identify problems and following this identification solutions and alternatives may be found.

David Kennedy completed his Masters at Birmingham University after working on a teacher training project in China. He is now working freelance.

4   From parliament to classroom: a question of quality

Corony Edwards

Introduction

The final case study in Section 1 looks at national changes in the politics and funding of education in the UK. It shows how those changes forced a further education college (for the post-16 age group) to revise its practices, and how its management implemented the changes, not entirely successfully. It is a fascinating study of two groups: one, the administrators, responsible for the management of the college; the other, the lecturers, undertaking teaching and learning. The case study looks at how the change upset the working balance between administrators and lecturers and led to conflict between the groups.

Change in education occurs frequently and at many levels, from the introduction of a new coursebook to the introduction of a new curriculum. The change may be instigated at the level of the classroom, by teachers and students, or may originate from a government initiative, or anywhere in between. This study aims in Part I to give a personal account of changes which took place within a college of further education in England that originated at least in part from national government. Management literature frequently refers to 'users' and their sense of ownership or rejection of an innovatory project. Part I is written from the viewpoint of a 'user' giving a narrative account of the introduction of change in her college, and how she and her teaching colleagues reacted to this, with a view to providing a vivid, if subjective, picture of events. In Part II the events described are examined in the light of some of the models and theories of change that have been put forward by various writers.

PART I

Background – government legislation

In the 1980s and 1990s, a number of UK government initiatives were taken affecting further education (FE) colleges in Britain (post-16 non-university education). One of the results was that all colleges became corporate institutions with charitable status and their own legal identity, funded by new National FE Councils for England and Wales. A greater emphasis was put on vocational training. New examinations were introduced in an attempt to bridge the academic/vocational divide. Non-vocational courses would be funded differently. In the past, funding had been based on the numbers of students enrolling on courses each academic year. The new arrangements would assess how many students successfully completed their courses, and payment would be made retrospectively. There was clearly pressure on colleges to increase the efficiency of their operations to maximize the 'success rate' and to put into place systems that would record and demonstrate that 'successful completion' had occurred. The documentary evidence, mainly in the form of records, was as important as the improvement itself.

These changes, introduced within a tight timescale, resulted in a flurry of activity on the part of college management, and at College X, where I was working, the force of this activity was felt. College X was one of the largest in the country with a full-time lecturing staff of over 300, about 600 part-time lecturers and over 10,000 students per year, many of them part-time.

Total quality management

The rise of TQM

References began to be made by senior staff in the college to 'Quality Management' and 'Total Quality' on staff information sheets and in minutes of meetings, following a large budget allocation by the college governors for a TQM (Total Quality Management) project. Most of the teaching staff appeared to pay little attention, perhaps believing that this was yet another of the transitory schemes of the management, and one which concerned only the latter in any case. However, the references persisted, and eventually the staff were told to attend an 'Awareness Giving Session' to explain what the term meant. It seemed that the college management were planning to adopt a TQM approach to their running of the college, and through this approach, to introduce procedures which would lead to BS5750 accreditation. (BS5750 is a set of procedures designed for industry, which if followed, are designed to ensure that a quality product is produced. Firms are inspected and if successful are awarded the qualification, which they can use as a mark of quality in selling their product.) Reaction in at least one faculty was extremely negative. Staff felt that their intelligence and professionalism had been insulted, that it was being implied that they currently did not do a good 'quality' job, and that they would be given yet more paperwork.

As time went by, more meetings, circulars and a leaflet entitled 'Your Guide to Quality and BS5750' were presented. There appeared to be little change in the attitude of staff towards the developments, and the proposed application for a British Standard in particular raised suspicion. This system would be acceptable as accreditation for a training provider to the relevant funding bodies, which was significant in that an increasing amount of work would be contracted to colleges which could prove that training of high quality could be provided. But lecturers did not seem to share the director's conviction that a system originally designed to monitor processes in the manufacturing industries could be applied to the teaching/learning situation. In one information-giving talk the director uncontroversially defined quality as 'fitness for purpose' but then went on to compare the students to pieces of raw iron entering a factory where various (Quality Controlled) processes would be performed on them until they emerged at the end of the course (production line?) transformed into gleaming new certificate holders. This did little to dispel lecturers' concern.

Consultation and communication

One of the key issues of Quality Management is that of consultation, through, for example, 'Quality Circles' – groups of elected or nominated individuals concerned with the processes to be monitored for quality. This part of the process had hitherto been left out, except for the reservation of a place on the Quality Management Committee for a representative of NATFHE (National Association of Teachers in Further and Higher Education), who attended on two occasions. At the request of NATFHE the project was delayed by six months while 'User Groups' investigated ways in which BS5750 could be implemented in their area. The members of these groups were selected mainly from middle management, and were supposed to consult staff and meet on a weekly basis to draft procedure documents. However, little consultation seemed to occur, and as some individuals belonged to more than one group, and all groups met at the same time, they could not have represented the views of staff in any case.

Communication did occur in other forms, but the direction was distinctly one-way, with memoranda signed by 'The Quality Management Committee' (membership was unidentified, rendering reply impossible) arriving regularly to inform staff of developments or instruct them to attend briefings. When large piles of draft procedure documents were delivered to all staff, covering every aspect of college administration (52 titles in all), for immediate implementation, dismay was apparent. Although many of the procedures were the same as had been followed by most staff for years, everything had to be recorded on the appropriate form and sent through precisely the right channel. When the video player broke, instead of telephoning the technician, who would call in later in the day to have a look, Document CQAP 09 (Control of Non-conforming Materials/Equipment Procedure) had to be consulted, and a 'Non-conformance label 38/1' had to be completed and attached to the offending item. The head technician would then be alerted, but before taking action would have to have any necessary repairs authorized by the Head of School (on yet another form) before sending a technician to do the job. The result: plenty of records of who had done what, when and how much it had cost, and no video player for a week. It was difficult to see how this constituted better quality; it looked far more like increased bureaucracy. While in times of financial constraint it is clearly important to have control over spending, it seemed that in this case the cost of staff time had been left out of the equation in many of the procedures suggested.

Auditing quality and overcoming resistance

Staff were told to make sure that all College Quality Documents, or CQDs (ie records) relevant to their area of work had been correctly completed in time for an internal audit. This was a dummy run for the first external audit, necessary for BS5750 accreditation to be granted. Some staff complied with the request; others ignored it. Then a letter was sent to the college management by three members of NATFHE, stating that 'whilst fully supporting the philosophy and implementation of processes which will improve the quality of what is delivered to the students' they were convinced that the timescale in which the new systems were to be implemented was totally unreasonable and should be slowed down to allow proper consultation and staff training to take place, and that the requirements of BS5750 were inappropriate to education and that this part of the scheme should be dropped.

As no satisfactory reply was given, a meeting and then a secret ballot were called, asking members to support the motion that they should 'refuse to co-operate with the new requirements of BS5750 and the audits shortly due to take place.' The outcome was that of a membership within the college of 315, 122 supported the motion and 80 voted against it. Members were instructed to politely refuse to co-operate when the auditors visited the college. Within days, a letter arrived from the director refuting NATFHE's claims and saying that staff who did not co-operate would be deemed to be in breach of their contracts, which state that staff are required to undertake ancillary duties related to their teaching programmes. The three individuals who had made the proposal to the union membership were asked to produce their records in another internal audit (no other staff were audited on this occasion), and because of their refusal to comply were given verbal and written warnings that they might be in breach of their contracts.

This action on the part of the director had the desired effect, because as the external audit progressed over the next few days, it became clear that staff were co-operating, and the dispute had collapsed. NATFHE wrote to all members informing them that the dispute was suspended because their prime objective was to protect the three members threatened with dismissal. The communication also expressed the concerns of the membership over the way that the matter had been handled and the future of the college: 'It is clear that despite the serious reservations expressed by the teaching staff, the director is determined to overcome any obstacle, by whatever means, in his quest for BS5750. Members and others must judge the value of accreditation when it has been achieved in such circumstances'; 'It is our remote hope that the director will recognize that this dispute has only resulted in an even more disenchanted staff whose present low morale cannot bode well for the unknown "total quality" that is the director's stated goal. Recent weeks have offered clear evidence of the director's personal and authoritarian style of management'; 'It is hoped that, if BS5750 is granted to this college, it will have been worth the money and time invested in the process. For many, the precise value of BS5750 remains something of a mystery as does its true cost' (internal NATFHE circular). A week later the director circulated a letter of congratulation to all staff on being the first college in the country to achieve Part 1 accreditation for BS5750.

PART II

An analysis of the innovation at College X

The preceding section has given a rather subjective account of the sequence of events during the implementation of one major change at College X, as viewed by the teaching staff (NATFHE members in particular). The following pages relate the pattern of events to some of the models of change that have been proposed in the literature.

Three approaches to managing change

Instrumental approaches

Slater (1985), in his survey of some of the major studies on the management of change, identifies what he describes as three rational approaches – instrumental, interactive and individual – where the components in the change process 'are normally identified as a series of sequential stages'. A commonly quoted example of an instrumental approach is the Research, Development and Diffusion (RD and D) model, where a rational series of phases develops new knowledge produced by research communities into usable products and services. The notion of 'managerialism', or the ability to change institutions from the outside, is central to this approach. Systems theory has a strong influence, in that the 'practitioners who were expected to embrace the projects were perceived as "systems", referred to in the literature alternatively as the user, receiver, adopter, or client systems.' (ibid). Instrumental approaches are essentially top-down and power-coercive in nature, with those in a position of power (at the 'top' or 'centre') imposing change on those in the lower levels of the hierarchy.

The change documented in this article does not fit the classic RD and D pattern, but the terminology and processes involved have much in common. The management of College X took an essentially instrumental approach, in spite of its claims to be following Total Quality Management practices with their promise of consultation and staff participation. It is notable here that the change sprang from new government policy on the roles of further education (ie greater emphasis on vocational training), with the changes effectively being enforced through new funding arrangements – very much a power-coercive strategy, even from a democratically elected government. Once translated into legislation, the diffusion or dissemination stage comprised the transmission of the new requirements to colleges through the Department of Education and Science, and college managements were then left to make their own decisions on how best to implement the changes.

According to Slater (1985), the final stage of such a process of change – the diffusion of the innovation from a centre out to its users – proves in practice to be the weakest link, occurring 'almost as an afterthought' (Becher and Maclure 1978, quoted in Slater 1985). Furthermore, the model assumes 'a consensus about values and goals that often does not exist in pluralist societies', and 'the bargaining powers of the users at the periphery relative to the centre give the former greater freedom to reject or modify the centre's designs'. Thus practitioners may fail to act as predicted or desired by development teams, limiting or even negating the impact of the projects.

At College X, the final stage contrasts somewhat with the classic RD and D model in that no materials or specific guidelines were provided as a result of the work of a national research team; rather, a general set of criteria were laid down for individual colleges to address in detail, for subsequent approval (or disapproval) by funding bodies. While this gives flexibility so that each college can fulfil the requirements in a manner appropriate to its local situation, it also assumes that the college managements have the expertise to do so. This is unlikely given the novelty of the requirements, hence the need for a substantial special budget item at College X, to buy in consultancy services, and/or employ new staff with relevant skills and train existing managers, in addition to the other costs of change.

It is also notable that while the government can adopt a power-coercive approach through legislation and gaining control of finances, so that colleges must either comply with the new legislation or go bankrupt, the managements of the colleges themselves do not hold the same level of power when they come to implement the necessary changes. In spite of this, at College X, the strategy was finally successful (at face value) since the director's implied threats of dismissal of staff who did not comply with the new requirements appeared to have the desired effect on the day of the external audit. However, as NATFHE's comments to its members imply, there is some question as to whether the award of BS5750 (Part 1) really means an improvement in quality of services and is valid as a guarantee of quality. Hurst (1983:16) recognizes that the result of such an approach is often 'token adoption'.

As a prescriptive model for managing change, instrumental approaches suffer from some major weaknesses. Although modifications and refinements have been made since their inception, Slater asserts that 'despite such modifications, by the mid 1970s there was general agreement among writers from various countries that, whatever the descriptive merits of instrumental approaches as characterized by the RD and D model with its centre–periphery assumptions, they were – without serious qualifications – seriously deficient as prescriptive models because of their lack of success in achieving change at the user level'.

At College X the change appeared to be successful at user level when staff co-operated in the audit. It may appear that the tax-payers get better value for money in that colleges are more accountable for the quality of the services they provide; possibly in political terms it would not be too cynical to say that the appearance is more important than the reality, since this is what will win votes. It is possible that the college management's aims were also mainly to do with appearances, particularly since the director seemed to be so anxious that College X should be the first FE college to gain BS5750 accreditation, in spite of the clear reservations of his staff. But the reluctance of the staff to be convinced that the change was indeed for the better suggests that wholehearted adoption will be unlikely. Although 'uncertainty avoidance' (Hofstede 1991) and 'dynamic conservatism' (Schön 1971, quoted in Slater 1985) are recognized phenomena, Slater points out that while 'dissent is characteristic of a "healthy" organization, conflict is indicative of a "diseased" organization'. The events at College X clearly fall into the category of conflict, and if Slater is right, this implies that the college has problems that run at a much deeper level than straightforward opposition to this particular change. Long-term low staff morale, negative attitude to management and strong opposition to a whole series of changes over the years, whatever their nature, would seem to support this suggestion.

Interactive approaches

As has been noted, the events at College X display many features of an instrumental approach, which Slater criticizes. Slater also describes the interactive approach, which attempts to overcome some of the deficiencies of an instrumental approach by shifting the focus towards social relationships, with dissemination being more prominent. A more active role for users is defined, with two-way communication allowing for the reaction of the users to be taken into account, even resulting in the abandonment of the project if reaction is strongly negative. In theory, such interaction is one of the features of TQM, although it has already been noted that real interaction was lacking at College X and the actions and rhetoric used by management were indicative of a one-way, top-down approach.

Hurst (1983) points out that participation is often a sham device used to manipulate users by making them *feel* that consultation has occurred. This is particularly so in educational establishments, where negative reaction is dismissed as 'conservatism' on the part of the teachers, who are blamed for the failure of a project which in industry would have been closed down to 'save throwing good money after bad' (Hurst 1983:56). One of the persistent complaints at College X was over the lack of genuine consultation. Even if the management felt that this *had* been provided (eg by offering NATFHE a place on the Quality Management Committee), the important point is that staff did not *perceive* this to have happened. The use of terms like 'Awareness *Giving*' and the presentation of plans as a *fait accompli* in the eyes of the staff all contributed to this. Although some kind of quality monitoring system was required by funding agencies, it did not have to be BS5750. The apparent attempt of management to adopt this particular system without presenting any alternatives suggests that management had in fact already made their choice in spite of the reaction of the staff, and the accusations of token consultation were justified.

Individual approaches

A third approach – individual – focuses on the specific nature of a local situation, or 'contextual variables', and the user is the starting point for problem-solving. Power equalization (ie giving the user an equal say in whether, and how, an innovation occurs) results in less opposition to the innovation being likely. The user, however, can be of any size or complexity (Slater 1985:453), so could be taken as anything from an individual teacher to the college or institution as a whole. A deeper level of analysis could see the institution as a sub-system, within which smaller users were identified. In the case reported here it appears that no users at any level were constructively involved during any of the stages of the innovation, and those who had to implement the change – the college staff – were certainly not the starting point.

In the case of the Further and Higher Education Act (1992), legislation was at least in part a response to problems identified by a business report 'Towards a Skills Revolution' (CBI 1990), which identified deficiencies in the education and training of young people in Britain. For example, they have fewer and lower qualifications than most of Britain's major European competitors. The innovation was motivated by a valid reason, but failed to recognize that involving college staff in solving this problem could result in successful change. Power equalization was not a feature of the method of finding a solution to these educational deficiencies nor of how the solution was to be implemented, either between government and colleges (as users) or teachers. Instead, the government set out three primary aims for resolving the deficiencies of post-16 education and training:

- to ensure that high quality education and training becomes the norm for all 16- and 17-year-olds who can benefit from it
- to increase the all-round levels of attainment by young people
- to increase the proportion of young people acquiring higher levels of skill and expertise

These aims, which reflected the government's preference for training as opposed to education, and were motivated by a concern for the economic health of the nation, were relatively uncontroversial. The method of achieving these aims, however, was more politically motivated, with changes being made in the control, funding and status of colleges, as described earlier. This pattern of events is strongly suggestive of an instrumental approach.

In contrast to the three approaches described above, Hurst (1983) suggests that it could be more useful to locate different approaches on a continuum, ranging from highly directive to highly non-directive approaches. The introduction of a quality system to a college as a result of government legislation can perhaps be better described if this hybrid model is used, with in this case a highly directive approach being adopted, both by government towards colleges, and in this instance, by college management towards staff.

Strategies for implementing change

Three types of strategy which describe the 'ragbag of various ploys and gambits which may or may not be helpful' (Hurst 1983:14) during the implementation of innovation are punishment and reward, change agent strategies and participation in decision-making by users. These have something in common with Bailey's (1982, quoted in Slater 1985:456) three competing 'systems of legitimation': the authority of management (essential if punishment and reward are to play a role), the conventions of democracy and the conventions of professionalism. The latter two demand participation in the process by users, which could be facilitated by a change agent, although such an agent could also represent the management in meting out reward and punishment. (For a fuller discussion of the role of the change agent, see Doyle in this collection.) These systems of legitimation were violated in the view of the teaching staff at College X, and that alone could provide sufficient grounds for opposing change.

The lecturers at the college viewed themselves as professionals rather than 'line-workers' in a factory or 'foot soldiers' (as they were referred to by a member of the management during one 'Awareness Giving' meeting), who had the right to be consulted on the jobs that they were to perform, and who felt that they were the ones who had the necessary expertise and experience to advise on how best to carry out the processes required by BS5750. They were suspicious of any type of change imposed from above, and were not prepared to accept either the right of the director to dictate the conditions of their jobs or the superficial explanations of the new systems that were designed to win them over to the idea. They did not feel that they had anything to gain from the new system, apart from unwelcome extra work, and co-operated only through fear of punishment (in the form of dismissal).

It is difficult to identify the change agent strategies employed in the College X project. The first 'Awareness Giving' meeting was conducted by a representative of the management, but met with a poor reception, and this procedure was dropped. In future meetings, either the director or one of his deputies spoke directly to staff. The information sent to staff originated either from the Quality Management Committee, the director, or the newly employed marketing director, the three appearing to work in close collaboration, so that management acted as its own change agent. Since one of the previous criticisms of management had been its inaccessibility and failure to communicate with staff, this approach was possibly an improvement, although staff did not seem to be any more positive in their response.

Conditions of acceptance

It has already been noted that the director of College X heralded the awarding of BS5750 Part 1 as a success, following the passing of the first external audit. It has also been suggested that the real success or failure of both BS5750 and the principle of Total Quality was yet to be seen. This ultimately depends on a number of factors, including seven conditions of acceptance:

- communication
- relevance or desirability
- effectiveness or reliability
- feasibility
- efficiency
- trialability
- adaptability   (Hurst 1983)

The superficial nature of the initial information on the requirements of the new system has been noted, although subsequently staff were inundated with lengthy and turgidly phrased procedure documents. These were in fact so inaccessible that few staff attempted to read them. In addition, the draft copies were recalled, and only key members of staff were to hold reference copies, so in fact the majority could not gain immediate access to find out what they should be doing even if they wanted to do so. Opportunities for feedback were limited and viewed as sham.

There was a strong feeling, reflected in NATFHE's circulars, that BS5750 was not only irrelevant, but also inappropriate, and was generally not feasible because of the administrative burden it would impose on staff who already felt under excessive pressure. The question of reliability, the apparent probability of the 'alleged benefits of the innovation actually accruing' is thus rendered meaningless.

If staff do not believe they can do what is required of them, or that in doing so they will negate any possible positive effects of a scheme, they are unlikely to believe it to be reliable. Whether the management of College X truly believed BS5750 to be a reliable way to ensure quality of provision, or whether it was seen to be a reliable means to some other end (prestige? continued funding?) is not known.

In some instances, procedures were demonstrably not feasible. For example, the 'turn-round' time for responding to enquiries about courses was impossible if all the stages were followed, because of the time it took to transfer paperwork from one office to another within the internal mail system. Time, simply to become familiar with the new requirements, was seen as the major problem. As Hurst (1983:59) points out,

UNIVERSITY OF NOTTINGHAM

SCHOOL OF EDUCATION

Receipt of Assignment/Dissertation

Candidate Name: .....Yuan Cheng (Cheryl).............

Course: ......MA ELTD.............................

Module Number: .....XXD 061.....................

Module Title: ....Learning to Learn............

For office use only

Date Received: ...31.05.02....... Signed: ....[signature]......

'participants need to accustom themselves to the new practice and iron out the snags. During the period of routinization, inputs of time are likely to need to be much greater than when the innovation is routine.' No extra time was made available for training or familiarization with procedures, which was an additional source of resentment from staff. Guaranteed efficiency and 'fitness for purpose' are the stated goals of BS5750, but while the system may provide a means of recording on paper that things have been done properly, staff felt that the time this would take would in fact lead to *less* efficiency and *poorer* quality, because the time would be better spent on teaching-related activities such as lesson planning or materials production. The rush to implement the requirements of BS5750 in time for the first audit, and to ensure that College X won the race to become the first in the country to receive accreditation, meant that trialability was an irrelevant issue. There was simply no time for trials, although most of the procedures and forms could have been piloted if time had been available.

Adaptability is an unknown quantity. 'Your Guide to Quality and BS5750' implied that changes should be made as part of the quality control process by following through the stages of the 'Corrective Action Cycle'. Adaptations 'include not only modifications to the innovation, but also in its context of use and in the potential adopters themselves' (Hurst 1983:59) so staff attitudes may also change. The following quotes, collected some two years after BS5750 was first awarded, give a flavour of how some staff felt, and the extent to which adoption or adaptation had occurred:

> In some areas, quality has improved, but this tends to be in the simple procedures, such as sending things to the reprographics unit.

> It's a 'paper' system. It hasn't addressed *real* quality. If anything, the quality of teaching is worse, because staff are so bogged down with paperwork.

> The system really just reinforces the quality we already have.

> I don't think the perceptions of the staff towards 5750 and TQM have changed since they were introduced.

The change process at the college has continued. It has received full BS5750 accreditation, ie Parts 1 and 2. The external audits were successful (although some surprise was expressed at this, as some staff who had been audited did not themselves feel they had satisfactorily carried out the prescribed procedures).

Conclusion

The failure of management to meet its responsibility to address any deficiencies in the conditions of acceptance can result in the failure of an innovation. However, any situation is complex, and any number of factors could lead to ultimate success or failure. There is, in fact, no single theory of managing change, just a host of parameters, only some of which have been mentioned above. For example, issues of acceptance/rejection behaviour such as cost/benefit analysis and decision-making processes have not been discussed here at all. Every situation will be different, and the parameters which operate will interact in different ways to produce different outcomes. It is for this reason that Hurst (1983:56) recommends that an innovative project be seen essentially as an experiment, with the main emphasis falling on project monitoring or implementation analysis. Analysis of the reasons for low levels of adoption should be followed by appropriate corrective action, requiring flexibility on the part of the management.

At College X, some kind of quality system must operate to satisfy funding agencies, so from a management point of view, the innovation may well be considered a success. Although the scheme was viewed with at best suspicion and at worst outright cynicism by the teaching staff, too much has already been invested to drop it only to try another which could prove equally unpopular. It is likely that the management at College X will work all the more determinedly to ensure continued accreditation. The difficulty will be in winning round the staff to at least make the best of what many would see as a bad deal, or to take an experimental view of the framework and work to adapt it so that it is more appropriate for an educational establishment.

It is possible that the management of College X decided to use power-coercive strategies to push through an urgently needed scheme to safeguard the college's financial health, with a view to monitoring and adapting the scheme using a more flexible approach, more in line with what is usually understood by TQM, once it was in place. My own feeling, however, is that the project was set off on the wrong foot; staff may do the minimum to allow future audits to be 'successful', which should satisfy the funding agencies, but that if there is any improvement in the quality of provision at the college it will have very little to do with BS5750. As with most administrative systems, there is plenty of scope for cheating, so token adoption will not be difficult. The 'guarantee' of quality it provides assumes that staff will not cheat, and that when problems are identified, the course of 'corrective action' chosen will in fact be appropriate. It cannot guarantee quality, but only that a set of procedures exist that, if followed, will set into motion activities designed to address any perceived problems. It is a sad irony that the nature of the system itself, with its heavy administrative burden, conspires to undermine the quality of provision at the college because of the demands made on staff and the negative attitude engendered.

It is true that the very negative account of events given in Part I is biased in that it gives a one-sided view – that of the principal users of the innovation – but as has been pointed out elsewhere, without user acceptance, an innovation is doomed to failure. It is interesting that Haigh (1992) quotes the 'American management guru behind the Japanese industrial miracle', Dr W. E. Deming, as rejecting appraisal, inspections, targets and incentives, instead favouring training, leadership and pride of workmanship: 'Quality is about people, not products'. In the same article, the head of a grant maintained school says of BS5750 that it 'seems inappropriate ... it's not central to the quality of what you're doing; it's simply getting the process approved by an external agency'. Management consultants are 'amusingly contemptuous' of developments such as BS5750 at a time when 'tight job descriptions and pay incentives are being phased out in industry'. In Haigh's words, 'Is education about to wade ashore on an island whence all others have departed?' If Deming and Haigh are right, then this puts a further nail in the coffin of BS5750 at College X. The introduction of an inappropriate, unreliable and outmoded quality assurance system in a college that shows many of the symptoms of a diseased organization, by a power-coercive management who have hitherto flouted many of the principles of a successful management of change, can only offer one real benefit: the important lessons it can teach us if quality at institutions like College X is really to be improved.

Appendix

Timetable of events

Month	Event
1	References to Total Quality Management first appear in notes on senior management team meetings circulated to lecturing staff at College X.
2/3	College governors allocate budget for a TQM project.
4	Paper 'Introduction to Quality Assurance; Total Quality Management; BS5750' circulated to all College X staff. Staff informed that the college is committed to implementation and are summoned to a meeting for explanation of basic concepts.
5	Government announces national funding council for FE colleges under direct government control.
7	Government announces all FE colleges to become corporate institutions in 2 years' time, to be funded by new National FE Councils for England and Wales, based on numbers of students *successfully completing courses*. Documentary evidence of this a prerequisite to funding.
5–14	Notes on senior management team meetings circulated to staff make regular reference to TQM and funding.
13	TQ information-giving meetings for staff – update on the implementation of the TQ system.
15	Staff attend a compulsory talk by college director on the implementation of a Quality Management System to satisfy BS5750 Part 1. Assistant directors nominate staff for across college user groups to review and evaluate procedures and identify necessary changes. Aim: to give ownership of changes to staff.
17	New Funding Councils set up. Interim (internal) audit to check that staff are using prescribed work procedures.
18	Drafts of College Quality Assurance Procedures and Operating Procedures circulated to all staff for comment and immediate implementation. Internal audits continue. NATFHE members request extended timescale for TQM introduction and proper consultation and staff training.
19	Dummy audit with external audit team.
20	Full college audit by external assessors. Director announces that BS5750 (Part 1) has been awarded.

Corony Edwards is a lecturer in English Language Teaching at the Centre for English Language Studies, University of Birmingham, where she is course tutor for the distance Masters programmes. She is currently researching the post-course impact of teacher training programmes.

2 Change in institutions

We now move closer to the level of implementation and consider changes taking place within institutions. All four articles in this section are less clearly influenced by changes occurring at national level, though like all change they are all in fact responses to changes occurring within the social context outside the institution concerned. Each article is written by a teacher who has been charged with introducing an innovation into classrooms and who is the professional link between the management of the institution wishing to introduce the change and the teachers implementing it in their classrooms. These change agents have various roles, such as director of studies and head of department.

Both the Doyle and the Pinar articles deal with the introduction of a new coursebook which represented a new way of thinking about language and methodology to the teachers concerned. Doyle describes the difficulty he had in implementing a decision to use a particular coursebook within his institution, and communicates the complexity of the situation. Doyle was fortunate in having a group of teachers who knew of the coursebook (though they had not used it in the classroom) and the theoretical approach underlying it as the result of attending related courses. They supported the decision to use it.

Doyle's problems began when he tried to convince teachers who did not have the same background of the book's benefits. He found it difficult to demonstrate the theoretical underpinning of the approach to those who had not been exposed to it. These 'resisters' perceived, whether correctly or not, that the choice had been imposed on them by management, and they also had practical teaching objections to the book. These reactions remind us once again of Ajzen's tripartite model of behavioural change (see Introduction and D. Kennedy's article in Section 1).

Doyle found it increasingly difficult to implement the policy as time went by. New teachers joined the institution who supported the resisters. Management changed so that the impetus behind the policy weakened, highlighting how fragile many innovations are and how dependent they are on individuals and their power and patronage. He does describe some tactical successes, however, and one in particular is instructive. During a familiarization session, he showed a video of the new methodology being used in a classroom. A participant who previously had found the approach difficult to conceptualize suddenly recognized its features from the video, characterizing it as 'project work' with which he was already familiar from L1 English secondary school teaching. He was able to match what he had seen on the video with something in his experience and the congruence of the two produced an insight and understanding which had not been possible before. He was able to conceptualize the innovation in his own terms, understood it, and became less resistant.

Doyle makes explicit that being a change agent responsible for implementation is a role demanding a complex combination of interrelated skills, including knowledge of language and of the teaching/learning process, management skills, and interpersonal skills. He concludes that in high-risk situations with a number of competing interests, interpersonal skills are crucial to managing the situation. This is particularly the case if you take a political rather than a rational view of change, the latter assuming that people will act in predictable ways if provided with relevant and appropriate information, the former that a situation is composed of competing interests where motives for actions will vary, in which unpredictable behaviour is likely and where conflict is inevitable but has to be managed if the innovation is to be implemented.

Pinar also describes the failure to introduce a new set of coursebooks into a school. Reading Pinar's description, the reasons for the failure are clear and the negative outcome predictable. The innovation was badly managed, partly due to the fact that there was no clear leader with power and influence co-ordinating the change, with the result that several people were taking different decisions without any overall strategy of change. There was little attempt to understand the teachers' objections to the materials and to negotiate some way forward. Teachers had strong reactions to the materials which they regarded as inappropriate and irrelevant for their needs and for those of their pupils. Communication between management and the teachers was poor, and no opportunity was given to the teachers to modify or adapt the materials, breaking a number of the conditions necessary for change.

Perhaps the greatest mistake the management made was to ignore those who were going to use the new materials, the teachers in the elementary school. The teachers realized that they were about to be asked to teach new materials only when they were presented with them at a meeting. Why management did this is not clear. It may be that the school had been run on hierarchical grounds with a strict division between management and teachers and that the former regarded decisions on materials to be within their area of expertise rather than that of the teachers. Whatever the reason, the result was predictable, with teachers rejecting the materials out of hand.

Despite this setback, Pinar describes how she learned (a theme of this collection) from the failure and tried again. This time, she brought teachers into the change process, giving information, answering their queries, and running training sessions. This time, the change was not forced, but teachers were encouraged over time to experiment with any aspects of the new materials they wished, integrating them with their existing practices. This seemed to create a more positive climate for change. Teachers were more ready to accept the new materials, though what is not clear from the description is how they taught them in their classes. Teachers may accept new materials as content to be taught, but unless we can observe how such materials are used, we cannot be sure that a methodological change has also occurred.

The remaining two articles in this section describe the challenges faced by change agents responsible for the introduction of new technologies in the classroom, in this case computer-assisted language learning (CALL) and the use of classroom video materials. Sergeant, working as a CALL co-ordinator in a language teaching centre in Singapore, gives a theoretical overview of the nature of CALL and the demands placed on someone like himself responsible for co-ordinating CALL activity within an institution.

Sergeant points out that CALL is still an additional rather than an integral part of the curriculum in most institutions and that it requires a high degree of teacher expertise. Without this expertise Sergeant argues that CALL remains at a low level of use within the curriculum in qualitative terms. In the institution Sergeant worked in, training was taken seriously and teachers had a variety of courses organized by the CALL co-ordinator. Collaborative activity appears to have developed too, with more experienced teachers helping the less experienced and teachers exchanging methods and materials. CALL can break down the normal barriers surrounding traditional classrooms where teachers tend to remain isolated from one another.

Sergeant believes that CALL constitutes a new sub-culture of learning with a 'people' system (teachers, students, managers) and a technology system (the hardware and software) in a network with the co-ordinator himself trying to keep the systems together. Sergeant emphasizes the learning aspect of the system, warning that there is a tendency to assume that once the technology is in place learning occurs through an unconscious process.

The success of the Singapore CALL system was due to teachers being given responsibility for it early on. They collaborated with one another and developed their skills together. How you create conditions where this self-learning occurs is not clear. According to Sergeant, such bottom-up developments, though beneficial, will not trigger major curriculum change, with full integration of CALL. Such far-reaching changes can only come with top-down direction. Without such changes, CALL may fossilize and may be restricted to a repertoire of traditional techniques which supplement rather than radically alter traditional activities used in the classroom.

The CALL co-ordinator plays a central role not only in providing assistance so that technical problems can be solved (the 'thing' level) but in attempting to introduce new practices among teachers and encouraging the institutionalization of these practices by management (the 'person' level). This reminds us of Doyle's description of change agent skills (subject matter, management, and interpersonal skills). Sergeant provides an informative outline of the activities a change agent needs to undertake both with managers and teachers in order to ensure the CALL facility works at the innovatory level he believes it should.

The value of Sergeant's article is in highlighting that the introduction of CALL is a more complex innovation than many have assumed, and in making us aware that what he says can be applied to any new 'technology' including materials or coursebooks. CALL appears on the surface to be a more complex system than materials or coursebooks, since the technical problems associated with CALL are clearly more evident (for example when a computer crashes). In fact the introduction of a textbook and the changes required to teaching and learning behaviours are as complex, just less apparent.

Bracamonte's article also deals with the introduction of new technologies, in this case both CALL and the use of video materials in the classroom. Not surprisingly perhaps, he found that the use of video materials was much easier and was widely accepted and implemented by teachers, whereas CALL met considerable resistance. Bracamonte explains the differential uptake of the two innovations by drawing on the conditions necessary for successful implementation, and comparing the two technologies against them. While video scores positively on almost all counts, CALL scores negatively. The perceived costs to the teacher of using CALL therefore outweigh the perceived benefits. In the case of video, benefits outweigh costs and the innovation was relatively easy to implement. Admittedly this says little about how the innovation was used by teachers in the classroom, only that it actually was used, something that we shall look at in Section 3.

The problem that was presented to Bracamonte, therefore, was how to introduce CALL when it was clear that it was not favoured by the majority of the teachers. In this situation, a change agent has three options: to drop the innovation; force it through using power structures; or devise a strategy to try to change perceived costs into benefits, using the skills that Doyle lists as part of the change agent's repertoire. Dropping the innovation is a possibility that should always be considered, since it may be the wrong time or the wrong context in which to introduce it. The change agent may feel that any attempt to change the balance from costs to benefits would not be realistic. It may also be that resisters are correct and that the change would not lead to improvement. Forcing the innovation is also a possibility and we saw an instance of this in the Edwards article in Section 1. We discussed the dangers of this approach if resistance is general and well-articulated. The third possibility is the one Bracamonte chose, creating a situation where benefits were regarded by teachers as more important than costs. He did this in a number of ways, all of which took time, an element of change we need to re-emphasize here. He used a type of cascade effect, setting up a group of teachers interested in CALL who were given training and who then passed on their training to other groups. From these further groups, a second group of trainers was selected who continued the work.

Key points

- Teachers' attitudes and beliefs must be considered.
- Attempts must be made to create positive conditions for change.
- Support from management is essential for successful implementation.
- Change agents have to maximize benefits and minimize costs to those implementing the change.
- Teacher expertise is crucial – this implies training.
- There is a possibility that a change may be implemented at a minimum surface level and may subsequently fossilize to a routine.
- It is important to build and create collaborative cultures.
- Change is as much a political as a rational activity.
- Change agents have to manage complex situations and require skills in subject content, management and interpersonal relations.

5

Changing course: the lexical syllabus and the politics of the staffroom

Paul Doyle

Introduction

As we have seen, an evaluation of the extent to which implementers' beliefs are compatible with any change, and a strategy if they are incompatible, are factors that change agents need to consider. Doyle's case study of the introduction of a new coursebook is no exception. However, Doyle also examines the political aspects of change. He believes there is a danger in describing change at a surface level without looking more deeply at the individuals and groups involved and what motivates their actions. Change involves a mix of power, influence, opinions, sympathies, sensitivities, and perhaps above all perceptions, all in a constant state of flux. Those involved in change, reacting to this mix of elements, will exhibit a whole set of behaviours. They may compete, co-operate, resist, lead, follow, sulk, plot, enthuse and so on, and change agents must try to manage these different elements and behaviours.

There is a chain of events in the life of an innovation that, properly exploited, leads to adoption. This case study explores the relationship between the research, design, marketing and publication phases of an innovation in English language teaching – the lexical syllabus – and the history of its adoption by the language centre where I worked in Singapore. The article focuses on the way in which new teaching materials replace old ones, and how this change is managed. In the case of the lexical syllabus, we can represent this as in Figure 1 below:

| Linguistic research | Syllabus design and course writing | Publication and marketing | Selection by school management | Adoption by teachers and students |

Figure 1: Implementation chain of events

I describe events leading to and following on from the adoption of the *Collins COBUILD English Course* by the language centre. The case study covers the period from 1987 to 1994. After a narrative account of my direct involvement from August 1988 to September 1992, I present an interpretation of these events using an essentially political framework (Buchanan and Boddy 1992). The aim of adopting such a framework is to clarify my role as a change agent, and to challenge the politically naive view of innovation assumed by some writers in the educational field.

Background

Innovation and the management of change processes in commercial language schools can best be understood by looking at management theory. One obvious reason for referring to the management theory literature is that commercial language schools are primarily motivated by profit. They are concerned with marketing their services effectively, providing a quality product for clients and customers, and competing with other similarly motivated organizations. Language schools are also relatively autonomous in their operations, unlike secondary schools which, in most countries, are responsive to government directives in areas such as curriculum development and examinations. Moreover, secondary schools generally do not compete with other secondary school systems and it is difficult to see them as profit-orientated. Innovation, in their case, is typically top-down and implemented on a nationwide scale, as Goh (this collection) observes in the Malaysian context. Comparisons with ELT organizations, therefore, can be rather tenuous.

Linguistic research and syllabus design

The core innovation of the *Collins COBUILD English Course*, the lexical syllabus, evolved from the corpus linguistic research being conducted by the COBUILD project team at Birmingham University in England. Sinclair (1987 and 1991) gives a thorough account of this work. The lexical syllabus and its role in the *Collins COBUILD English Course* are described in Renouf (1987), Sinclair and Renouf (1988) and Willis (1990). Carter and McCarthy (1988:160), in a discussion of Sinclair and Renouf (1988), observed that: 'A coursebook based on this syllabus would be radically different from conventional ones and would almost certainly meet resistance at first'. Renouf herself highlighted problems during the early stages of production of the course materials when she noted difficulty in reconciling findings with received notions: 'We were anxious about the likelihood of a similar reaction among colleagues in language teaching who would not have had the same opportunity to see the facts demonstrated for themselves.' (1987:177). Willis (1990:vi), in a detailed account of how the course materials were prepared, mentions initial concerns about ease of use for teachers:

> At first we had doubts about the practicality of the lexical syllabus. But the more we worked with the information supplied by the COBUILD research team the more we became convinced that the syllabus which emerged was highly practical, entirely realistic and vastly more efficient than anything we had worked with before.

The key point here is that access to the research data alone appears to be convincing, even to specialists.

Publication and marketing

In 1987, Collins published level 1 of the *Collins COBUILD English Course*. The blurb on the back of the Teacher's Book proclaimed a new approach to course design, which:

> ... represents a major advance in the teaching of English. It is based on the research findings of the COBUILD project at Birmingham University – the same research which produced the acclaimed *Collins COBUILD English Language Dictionary*. It focuses on the real English students will encounter and need to use in today's world.

Much of the advertising material for this innovative set of language-teaching materials emphasized the authoritative nature of the contents, 'the real English students will encounter and need to use in today's world.'

Publication, however, is not implementation. We need to look very closely at the circumstances surrounding a specific attempt to adopt the new syllabus in an actual context if we are to gain useful insights about the politics of the implementation process.

The next section documents key events in the implementation process from the point of view of an individual responsible for the management of the innovation, a change agent. It also presents a description of the institution, its management structures and other factors relevant to the analysis.

Selection and adoption

The authors of the *Collins COBUILD English Course*, both graduates of Birmingham University, worked in close association with the COBUILD project and its research data. They wrote and piloted the materials while working in Singapore, one of the authors being the director of the language centre where I worked from 1983 to 1986. Both gave in-house workshops to teachers on the COBUILD research and the work in progress.

In 1987, the manager responsible for the General English Unit and the senior teacher responsible for General English courses, both holders of the MA in Applied English Linguistics from Birmingham University, planned and implemented the introduction of the *Collins COBUILD* level 1 course on elementary part-time courses on a trial basis. At least two other teachers were studying on masters degree courses at Birmingham during this period, and this situation continued until 1992.

Several of the management and teaching staff at the centre were familiar with the COBUILD project. They were largely sympathetic to the promotion of lexis to a new level of importance, to corpus-based linguistics, and to products based on the research. The language centre was, therefore, in a uniquely favourable position to innovate in terms of awareness of the lexical syllabus and close contact with the research.

After a successful move to new premises in 1987, the language centre's business grew steadily. At the same time it diversified its services. It operated as four units, the largest being the General English Unit (GEU), each offering an increasing range of course types. This led to delegation of decision making, financial planning and marketing processes from the director to the managers of each unit. In addition, distinctive sets of courses or clients were seen as the responsibility of a senior teacher who initiated and co-ordinated further course development. This was typically realized as a project, with the senior teacher heading a course team of several teachers.

Between 1987 and 1992, therefore, the language centre can be seen as an organization in transition from a role to a task culture (Handy and Aitken 1986). A role culture is one where job function and senior management determine who can do what in the organization. White (1988) has observed that language school chains tend to be role culture organizations. In contrast, a task culture is job or project orientated. It forms cross-functional teams who can best solve the problems related to a particular job or process. One of the organizational structures used at the language centre is the course team, a group of teachers who teach on the same course and meet regularly to discuss teaching issues for that course. With a team, Handy and Aitken state:

> … a group or team of talents and resources are applied to a project, problem or task. In that way each task gets the treatment it requires – it does not have to be standardized across the organization – and the groups can be changed, disbanded or increased as the task changes. (Handy and Aitken 1986:88)

The formation of course teams at the language centre suggests, as Handy and Aitken indicate, an emerging task culture.

The next section contains my account of the attempt to implement a lexical syllabus at the language centre. The aim is to provide ethnographic data similar to the diary studies mentioned in Buchanan and Boddy (1992). The 'texture' of the language school environment, to use Buchanan and Boddy's terminology, is most tellingly felt in staffrooms, where the crucial mores and shared values circulate virtually unrecorded. I will argue that it is only this kind of data which proves useful in understanding events and developing practical guidelines for change agents.

Change agent's account

1988
I joined the language centre as a teacher, transferring from Jakarta, where I had worked as an assistant director of studies. In Jakarta, the *Collins COBUILD* course materials had been reviewed for possible use on general English courses but rejected on the grounds that they were too ethnocentric and too complicated to use. I recall one staffroom discussion that focused on the cassettes supplied with the course, which were 'impossible to use'. Discussion amongst teachers was generally negative and the materials were never adopted.

July 1988
When I arrived in Singapore, the *Collins COBUILD* course materials had also been considered, but here the story was very different from Jakarta. The materials had been introduced on a trial basis for elementary part-time courses and were being readied for full-time courses. It was common knowledge among teaching staff that the GEU manager and senior teacher aimed to introduce the level 2 materials when they were published. This subsequently occurred during July 1989. Towards the end of 1989, the GEU manager left Singapore and the senior teacher was promoted to fill this position. I was promoted to senior teacher position.

July 1989
The *Collins COBUILD* course was deemed a failure on the elementary part-time course and replaced by *The Cambridge English Course.*
Reaction to the perception that the *Collins COBUILD* course was officially sanctioned and favoured set in.

January 1990
As a result of promotion, I entered a position of responsibility and power during the early stages of implementation. At the same time, the responsibilities of all senior teachers were restructured, and I became responsible for all full-time courses in the GEU. This reorganization of job responsibilities had repercussions later, as will be seen. *Collins COBUILD* level 2 was introduced on intermediate full-time courses.
Growing opposition amongst teachers was apparent in staffroom discussions with the senior teacher; many reasons were reported. Course teams meetings were held to allow expression of grievances.

September 1990
Willis' *The Lexical Syllabus* was published.

1991
In-service training sessions were held on basic *Collins COBUILD* course elements: research findings (lexical syllabus) and methodology (task cycle), and alternatives to the Present–Practice–Production shape for lessons.

There was a loss of staff experienced with *COBUILD* from course teams, partly due to timetabling changes.

High turnover of staff meant an influx of *Collins COBUILD* course–inexperienced teachers to add to the pool of resistance, and led to demands on the senior teacher to repeat training, clarification, etc.

The question of the *Collins COBUILD* course generating too much work for the senior teacher in terms of training was raised by the GEU manager at a meeting.

The account given above highlights important features of the context. It is a retrospective summary, and inevitably subjective. Nevertheless, it does reveal aspects of the 'phenomenological texture of the context' (Buchanan and Boddy 1992:44), or the nature of change as it was experienced by the change agent.

Interpretation

Marketing innovation: the failure to educate users

Most writers on change emphasize the need to educate the eventual end users of an innovation. Unlike previous innovations in ELT syllabuses, however, the *COBUILD* coursebooks came to market with little published or disseminated information preceding them. It was relatively difficult, therefore, for change agents to facilitate a 'smooth' implementation because they had not acquired the expertise that comes from experience of working with new teaching materials. The lack of this expertise was clear in the language centre when I arrived there: none of the initial advocates among the centre's management had taught the materials, although they were knowledgeable about the new concepts incorporated in the course. I am making a distinction here between practical and conceptual expertise. By teaching the *Collins COBUILD* course, a change agent gains practical expertise which enables him or her to deal with teachers' questions, doubts and resistance, and from a credible standpoint.

The publication of *The Lexical Syllabus* (Willis 1990) could have contributed to the 'educational' aspect of marketing the three-book set of course materials. Willis' account is convincing, clearly argued and supported by numerous examples from the published course materials. The practical value of *The Lexical Syllabus* as a source of basic facts for those involved in preparing teachers to use the *Collins COBUILD* coursebooks is clear, but it was published too late to realize that value. The author of the *Collins COBUILD* course was clearly aware of the radical nature of his approach and the need for a new way of teaching the materials. Notions of learner training and the learner as discoverer are suggested as the most effective way for students to learn. But this had far-reaching implications for teachers:

We are much more likely to realise this ideal if we abandon the idea of the teacher as 'knower' and concentrate instead on the notion of the learner as 'discoverer.' ... It is to be hoped that techniques which specify a learner's corpus, and provide learners with a framework within which to examine that corpus, will enable teachers to place learners at the centre of the learning process. (Willis 1990:131)

As has already been argued, knowledge of the COBUILD research findings is necessary to overcome doubts about ease of use and the effectiveness of the course materials. Yet this knowledge was lacking amongst practitioners in Singapore. As a result, teachers were disadvantaged in their traditional role of 'knower' and inexpert in the role demanded of them by the new materials. The crucial questions for a change agent, therefore, became: how are teachers to acquire the new expertise? How are they to develop an awareness of the learner as 'discoverer' if they are comfortable with their role as 'knower'?

It is possible to take an alternative point of view and say that there is nothing in the *Collins COBUILD* course that a professional teacher would not be able to cope with, as long as they were prepared to take risks in the classroom and keep an open mind about the language. This appeared to be the response of the course writers to a set of prepared questions gathered from teachers at the language centre in Singapore. The challenging nature of the materials were an indication of their value to the profession. This is a naive position, however, in terms of managing innovation. All staffrooms have a mix of more or less experienced teachers with differing qualifications and, most importantly, personal theories of language acquisition and learning. Unless they are carried along by a pioneering spirit, perhaps only truly possible if access to the research and data is feasible, it is unlikely that they will simply jettison the methods, beliefs and values on which they have built their professional careers.

The *COBUILD* set of course materials included a detailed Teacher's Book, with extensive notes on each task, unit and the course methodology and design as a whole. However, I would argue that a Teacher's Book alone cannot be considered an effective vehicle to prepare teachers for such a radical innovation. The normal vehicle for such preparation in a language school would be some form of staff development programme, including such strategies as regular training workshops, lesson observations and counselling sessions, with perhaps an initial meeting to present information and allow discussion of the issues. Some of these strategies were available to me in the form of in-house workshops held every week and a management policy of at least two observations of every teacher by senior teachers or unit directors a year.

Change agent solutions

The important thing here is not the solutions that I came up with (see Figure 2 on p60), many of which are familiar training activities to most in-service teacher trainers and senior teachers. More cogent is the interpretation of these solutions with the assumption that the change agent is *creatively* trying to make the innovation process succeed. Some methods are clearly practical and neutral in terms of dealing with inadequacies in the original implementation; others are more recognizable as political strategies, used in a struggle against opponents to the change process.

- Interviewing the author: presenting to the course writers prepared questions collected from a few teachers regarding practical problems, and circulating the answers among all teachers.

- Presentation of material from *The Lexical Syllabus* and the *Collins COBUILD* Teacher's Book in more palatable form in the teachers' course notes.

- Rewriting teachers' course notes to include information reporting on accumulated experience of teaching in a chatty style to increase user-friendliness.

- Re-chunking syllabus to ensure teachable sequences in each daily lesson.

- Using alternative arguments to deflect criticism (for example, identifying the problem of too many teachers sharing the same course leading to co-ordination difficulties: 'You're having difficulty teaching the course because it's difficult for the three of you to liaise. That's a timetabling problem, not one with the materials.').

- Identifying key supporters and amplifying their successes.

- Using humour in the face of setbacks; being enthusiastic about the materials; being helpful to those with problems and spending more time than normal with them.

- Re-planning whole full-time programme: substituting popular coursebook at low intermediate level, and moving unpopular level 2 coursebook to upper intermediate level to replace another unpopular coursebook.

- Turning resistant teachers' arguments on their head: students' grammatical accuracy doesn't improve because we have exaggerated beliefs about acquisition.

- Videoing myself teaching to demonstrate students having fun whilst learning with the materials.

- Using different terminology: for teachers with secondary school experience, task based teaching is 'project work'.

- Identifying possible reasons why some teachers liked the materials: for example, secondary school training seems to predispose teachers to the course.

- Inviting teachers to watch me teach and later discussing how-to-teach issues.

- Holding in-house workshops for all teaching staff to highlight differences between the *Collins COBUILD* course's task-based approach and the conventional 'Present–Practice–Production' methodology.

- Conducting two in-house workshops a week instead of one, to ensure more people can attend and therefore to amplify solutions.

- Building up video and computer based activities to challenge issue of 'no supplementary materials'.

- Promoting use of the *Collins COBUILD* Practice Book in class for extra controlled practice activities to tackle the claim that there was 'no grammar in the course'.

Figure 2: Selling the *COBUILD* materials – solutions tried by change agent

Weathering the storm – turbulence and fuzzy structures

Management has been characterized as 'operating in turbulent field', that is, managers face a highly complex and rapidly changing environment (Buchanan and Boddy (1992). Organizational structures can be seen along a cline between mechanistic, rigid, routinized structures and organic, fluid, adaptive structures. Other terms that have been used are 'crisp' and 'fuzzy' respectively. The underlying metaphor in these descriptions is that of flow and growth, with 'turbulence' having a dual meaning. The relationship between the inner and outer contexts of an organization – between a business and its arena of market forces, competitors and the wider economic world situation – can be turbulent, and the process of change itself can result in turbulence within an organization.

It is interesting, in passing, to note the importance of this particular metaphor to Rinvolucri, a well-known innovator in the field of English Language Teaching, in his first-hand account of resistance to change (Rinvolucri 1981). Discussing inner resistance to new ideas as an indicator of significance, he describes a conflict between previous knowledge that we heavily invest in and whatever is new:

> This causes something in my mind akin to the turbulence one sometimes gets while flying: I am buffeted and thrown around without being able to clearly see the reason why, at the time, that is. The clarity of hindsight is all too easy. (1981:47)

In writing this article, I am conscious of trying to impose a regular framework on what was essentially a 'turbulent' sequence of events. Rinvolucri's personal account and the more formal analysis by Buchanan and Boddy provide a more accurate characterization of the period of innovation reported here. Their analysis corresponds well with that of White et al. (1991) who, as we have seen, remark on the 'fragmented structure' of schools.

Organizational structure

Schools and language centres are complex organizations. One reason for this is the relative lack of organizational structures, what some observers have described as a lack of 'collegiality' (White et al. 1991). Teachers spend most of their professional lives alone in their classrooms with their students. As a result, they are typically unavailable for formal meetings unless these are scheduled into the school timetable, and normally grab opportunities for informal discussions in their breaks. More importantly perhaps for a discussion of innovation, they are cut off from *each other* unless practices such as team teaching or peer observation are sanctioned by the school. This leads to a fragmented management and communication structure, which reduces the opportunities for involving teaching staff in decision-making processes (1991:167). This point is worth considering further: as we shall see, the degree to which the recipients of innovation have *ownership* of change is often considered crucial for successful implementation, and depends in part on participative management.

Texture and expertise

Concepts such as the 'expertise of change agents' and the 'texture of the organizational context' are especially relevant and valuable because they help us to situate innovations within the socio-political background where they inevitably occur. Studies that, at one end of the spectrum, encompass writings such as Toffler (1992) and, at the other end, research-based analyses such as that by Buchanan and Boddy (1992) provide insights that more narrowly focused educational observers do not. The use of diary studies by Buchanan and Boddy to get inside the change process and observe how change agents themselves perceive their role, allows us a clearer understanding of the key concepts 'expertise' and 'texture'.

Arguing against a simplistic interpretation of organizational structures and processes, Buchanan and Boddy take up a quite different position, based in part on their diary studies of change agents operating in various business contexts in the late 1980s. They make a distinction between the 'public performance' of the change agent, and what they refer to as 'backstage activity', and this theatrical metaphor enables them to develop a more sophisticated analysis of change agent expertise. Their central argument is that:

> ... the change agent has to support the 'public performance' of rationally considered and logically phased and visibly participative change with 'backstage activity' in the recruitment and maintenance of support and in seeking and blocking resistance. The public performance typically follows the ritual and legitimating script of the rational–linear model of project management. 'Backstaging' is concerned with the exercise of 'power skills', with 'intervening in political and cultural systems', with influencing, negotiating and selling, and with 'managing meaning'. This is achieved in a *creative* way, through appropriate symbolic actions in attempts to legitimize change by suggesting different and new interpretations of events inside and outside the organization. (1992:27)

In the light of this analysis, it is possible to re-interpret some of the solutions listed in Figure 2 on p60. The powerful role of video, which has been noted by Rudduck (1990), enabled me to exploit a difference in terminology that had its roots in a difference in training backgrounds. A number of teachers at the language centre had previously trained as secondary school teachers of English. When shown a video of my students working enthusiastically on a task involving the preparation of a tourist poster for their own country, these teachers identified what they saw as 'project work'. The significance of this term, from their earlier training, helped them to accommodate a new perspective on the *Collins COBUILD* course: the course had legitimacy in their eyes now that they had *named* one of its components. Through naming, they were able to take ownership of the innovation.

In subsequent course team workshops, I employed this video ostensibly to discuss which tasks were successful on the course and which were not, but with an awareness of the potency of combining images of students having fun with an interpretation of a task-based methodology as project work. This is an example of 'managing meaning' through symbolic action:

> ... the change agent's use of familiar, traditional and acceptable organizational procedures to promote the dismantling of other organizational arrangements and the introduction of the new.' (Buchanan and Boddy 1992:25)

I had decided that the course team meeting, with its apparently more practical 'fix the leaks' image, was a better vehicle for in-service training than the in-house workshop forum, which had become associated with unwelcome new ideas from management and, consequently, was poorly attended.

Buchanan and Boddy identify three agendas the change agent must have expertise in to manage change effectively:

1 content – substance of changes implemented

2 control – planning, monitoring techniques

3 process – communication, negotiating, and the management of enthusiasm and resistance

They also focus on four dimensions in which the context or 'texture' is experienced by the change agent and which contribute to the degree of 'personal vulnerability' for the change agent:

1 shifting sands (changing inner and outer context for the organization)

2 interlocking (dependence on other staff, managers and suppliers)

3 ownership

4 senior stance (attitude of senior management to the innovation)

The variations possible can be seen in Figure 3 on p64. Buchanan and Boddy conclude that the priorities given to the three agendas above depend on the vulnerability of the change agent. In high vulnerability contexts a change agent is advised to proceed in a manner that resembles a rational–linear model of change, but at the same time to conduct significant 'behind the scenes' action. Change agents who have a limited understanding of the content of the innovation but who are strong in team building, communicating and other process skills can be effective in high vulnerability contexts.

One problem with the introduction of the *Collins COBUILD English Course* at the language centre in Singapore was the radical nature of the research findings it was based on. Not having had the opportunity that researchers and writers had to work with the research data seriously compromised any attempt to appeal to teachers' rational acceptance of the materials as a methodological step forward. Such a strategy relies on the consumers of innovation being able to comprehend the content of any change. In retrospect, it was an easy step to predict that those with less specialized knowledge – teachers – would experience serious difficulty using a lexical syllabus. They needed more than the notes in a teacher's book to help them change course. The authors' own guide to the course was published three years after the first level of course materials, by which time it was too late to be of much use.

As I became responsible for the maintenance of the full-time courses affected by change during the trial period for the *Collins COBUILD* course, I had to tackle a multitude of issues before I had actually taught the course. Thus at the same time as being cast in the role of change agent, being the one responsible for the new coursebooks, I was also subject to the change process myself. Moreover, I had as little experience of the research findings as most new teachers in the centre.

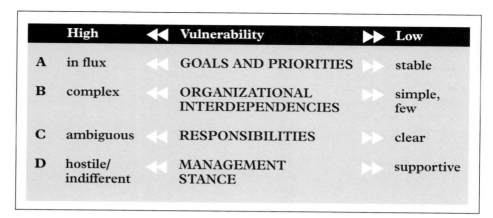

High	◀◀ Vulnerability	▶▶ Low
A in flux	◀◀ **GOALS AND PRIORITIES** ▶▶	stable
B complex	◀◀ **ORGANIZATIONAL INTERDEPENDENCIES** ▶▶	simple, few
C ambiguous	◀◀ **RESPONSIBILITIES** ▶▶	clear
D hostile/ indifferent	◀◀ **MANAGEMENT STANCE** ▶▶	supportive

Figure 3: Contextual factors determining 'vulnerability' of change agent

To illustrate this, I would characterize my vulnerability during the implementation period under discussion as:

A Neutral   My goal was to introduce the course successfully; my priorities were to get the job done and introduce levels 2 and 3.

B Fairly high   Each *COBUILD* teacher has allegiance to several courses and senior teachers, and groups of students.

C High   No performance management system, no real authority invested in senior teacher position.

D High   Management becoming increasingly indifferent.

Team building, communication and 'process' skills make up the expertise that I had to develop in Singapore, where a number of factors contributed to a fairly high degree of vulnerability in the context. There was a gradually increasing indifference by management to the *Collins COBUILD* course as the author–manager moved on. The original change agent became a unit director concerned with issues such as delay in books arriving, complaints from teachers and time spent on orienting new teachers to a 'difficult' coursebook. To a certain extent my responsibilities were ambiguous in that I had not introduced the course. I took over a trial period with no clearly defined evaluation criteria or timescale for the project.

One could argue that organizational interdependencies in an English language centre are fairly complex. It is a common perception of new teachers that it is a large and confusing place with too many types of course and kinds of student, complicated administrative systems, and even too many bosses to contend with. Much of the organizational structure tends to rest on the different kinds of students being taught and the courses developed for them, the times when they are taught, meetings to sort out practice exams, trips, absences and all the usual administration of a busy language centre or school. Other key aspects of the role that I developed are listed below.

Focusing on key opinion makers and holders
- damage control
- marshalling supporters

Training in new techniques
- highlighting syllabus words with a highlighter pen
- integrating dictionary use into lessons
- hunting for examples of syllabus items in other units
- ways of reporting back in a task-based lesson

Counter-attack
- highlighting the problem of the multi-syllabus being common to all materials
- focusing on weaknesses in other coursebooks

Metaphorical attack
- isolating the mechanistic metaphors teachers use to talk about language learning and what they do, in order to raise awareness of underlying theory
- using the alternative organic metaphor to argue with people
- engaging in symbolic action in order to change the image of the job

Attitude attack
- putting yourself at risk: asking questions such as, 'Is the teacher the expert?' and 'Shouldn't the customer decide if the coursebook is boring?', thereby fostering conflict through open argument (Buchanan and Boddy 1992:26)

Conclusion

What is emphasized in this kind of analysis is the importance of managing political aspects of the change process and the attempt to gain legitimacy for the innovation itself. What a mere sequence of events tends to omit is the ebb and flow of political forces within a staffroom. The change agent may have to contend with a small, sceptical group of resisters who can influence the opinion of participants in a change process. Buchanan and Boddy are right to point out the inadequacies of the 'truth, trust, love and collaboration' approach to change (1992:14), and to outline methods for the creative manipulation of elements within the context (including participants' views and perceptions). A collaborative approach which does not take on board the 'whole person' of the participant is essentially politically naive.

Paul Doyle has taught English in India and Sudan, and has worked for the British Council in Sudan, Indonesia and Singapore. He is a senior training consultant in the British Council's Business Communication Centre in Singapore, responsible for designing training programmes for corporate clients, and running workshops in selling, presentation, negotiation and interpersonal skills.

6   Introducing new course materials

Kemale Pinar

Introduction

None of the case studies so far has shown the implementation of change to be an unqualified success. Change is complex and means many things to the people involved. The change that Pinar describes, the adoption of new coursebooks in a school in Saudi Arabia, satisfied no one at all. No group – parents, pupils, administrators, teachers – appeared to gain and at the first attempt the change was not implemented. There are, however, two positive aspects to this case study. One is that by analysing retrospectively why the change failed, those involved could use different strategies in the future, and indeed a second attempt to introduce the materials was more successful. The other is that the teachers did have the power to reject the change, which in the circumstances was probably the correct decision, and the management wisely decided not to force the issue.

The purpose of this case study is to describe an attempt to change the course materials used in a school and to investigate the reasons which led to the failure of the effort. It is assumed that the outcome of this investigation will provide proof in support of the importance of management in the implementation of change.

In the first part of this article, issues which may be crucial in determining the success or the failure of educational changes will be discussed. In the second part, the process of change will be described, starting with the conditions which prompted the change. The events which took place during the implementation stage and the reasons which caused the rejection of the change will also be explored in this section. In the third part, the situation that emerged after the failure to implement the proposed change will be examined and some possible solutions will be proposed to help solve the problems which were encountered during the process.

Why do innovations fail?

Most teachers have had to implement educational changes which are macro-level changes. This simply means that when an innovation is being planned, decisions are made at top levels and the changes are carried out at lower levels or by external agencies. The problem with such an approach is that the people who will be most affected by the changes are often excluded from the process. As a result of this, resistance towards the change develops during the implementation process (Hurst 1983, Young and Lee 1985, and Bolam 1976). Pettigrew (cited in Buchanan and Boddy 1992) argues that for effective change in an organization it is necessary to have 'involvement, participation, ownership, communication, commitment, and trust'. The concept of establishing ownership of the project is seen as a central issue. The participants' involvement in and contribution to the events and outcomes is assumed to be the solution to the problem of resistance.

It is also possible to find arguments against participation as a strategy. The argument is that participation in decision-making may have undesirable outcomes. Slater (1985) cautions us that participation in decision-making may release forces in favour of conservation rather than change. Sometimes the participants may not be willing to take part in the decision-making process because of lack of expertise in their field, or a lack of motivation. Some teachers, for example, might be reluctant to volunteer the time needed to take part in working groups, as they may not want to spend extra time working on such projects after normal working hours. In such cases, participation may even have a negative effect on the outcome. Bolam (1976) argues that not all teachers are innovative and claims that a participatory structure in a school which contains a majority of traditionally minded staff will probably not be innovative. Projects may not succeed because a group of teachers do not want to change the way they are used to doing things. If people are genuinely allowed to participate in decisions concerning innovations, they may oppose the change or even veto it.

An alternative solution to this problem comes from Hurst (1983) who suggests that rather than allowing for wider participation, the views of all interest groups should be taken into consideration when implementing innovations. Hurst claims that such an approach may reduce error in decisions that are taken and diminish the unfair distribution of benefits that is likely when only one interest group monopolizes such decisions.

Another important factor in the process of change is the attitudes of the people involved. People by nature tend to feel threatened by whatever is unfamiliar to them. They prefer to cling to the old and the familiar to protect themselves from unpleasant consequences. Teachers are no exception to this. Nonetheless, they often find themselves in situations where they are expected to adopt new ideas, new methods of teaching or new teaching materials in a short space of time. Teachers' reactions to such demands may differ greatly. Some may agree with the changes and accept to follow them. Others may choose to resist them in order to avoid failure which might result from accepting the changes. It is also possible that teachers do not show initial resistance to the change. Instead they simply ignore the changes. In a study reported by Gross et al. (cited in Bolam 1976) it was observed that although there was no initial resistance to the innovation, the degree of implementation was minimal. The reasons for this lack of success are identified as:

1 The teachers did not have a clear understanding of what was expected of them in their new role.

2 They did not have the necessary skills to carry out their new role.

3 They did not have the required materials and equipment.

4 There were no feedback procedures to correct these deficiencies.

Young and Lee (1985) state that 'information about a new way of teaching and one's understanding of the principles underlying it are an important source of attitude change'. The authors propose two options – either to try to change teachers' attitudes or to accept the stability of teachers' attitudinal norms in a given society and devise an efficient curriculum around those norms rather than attempting to change them.

We shall see in the next section how these facts played a part in the case study described.

Case study

The attempted change took place in a private school in Saudi Arabia where I taught English for many years. The school provides education from nursery through to twelfth grade and has about seven hundred pupils, all girls, between the ages of 3 and 18.

The English department staff is made up of 15 non-native teachers who come from diverse educational backgrounds. The teachers also show diversity in the years of experience they have had teaching EFL and in their beliefs and attitudes towards language teaching. The English department is divided into two sections: elementary (kindergarten–6th grade) and secondary (7th grade–12th grade). Each section is supervised by a senior teacher or head of department. The senior teachers provide support and guidance to the teachers in educational and administrative matters, check lesson plans and monitor the exam questions set by the teachers, observe classes and deal with students' problems related to learning English. The senior teachers also play an important role in the selection of course materials to be used in each section.

English is an important part of the curriculum and the strength and the effectiveness of the English course is an important factor when parents select a school. The English curriculum for the elementary school is set by the school with the approval of the local education authorities. At secondary level two different programmes are followed: the compulsory government programme and the supplementary school programme. Students are offered six to nine periods of English according to their class level.

Two sets of books were in use at each class level in the elementary section. One of these was an EFL coursebook designed to teach English to young learners. The second book was a reader originally prepared for learners with reading difficulties. The EFL coursebooks were structurally graded and they emphasized mastery of the lexico-grammatical patterns of the language. The programme was primarily concerned with improving speaking skills. Reading and writing were almost totally ignored in the first three coursebooks.

The effectiveness of the English curriculum in the elementary section had been a major source of concern for a number of years. As a direct result of using materials which emphasized learning of the grammatical structures over meaningful language use, progress among learners was slow. The beginner students had problems in expressing themselves as well as in reading and writing. The more advanced learners, who knew some English when they joined school, were demotivated because the language activities in the English classes did not interest them. Reading and writing constituted a problem for these students as well.

Readers had been introduced to add some content to the programme and to overcome the problems related to reading. The books were first tried with a group of beginner students at the 7th grade. When this experiment was successful, the readers were given to all classes in addition to the EFL materials.

The readers did not produce the same effect at the elementary school level as they did with the trial group. Most teachers found the readers difficult to use in their classes. They continued using the EFL materials, most of the time avoiding the readers as much as they could.

Another problem in the elementary section was related to management. Many changes took place at the administrative level as well as among the teaching staff. This situation created instability, and problems which needed to be solved immediately remained unsolved.

At the beginning of the school year the senior teacher of the elementary section resigned unexpectedly. I was asked to help the new senior teacher at the elementary section as I had taught for many years at this section before transferring to the secondary section. My informal advisory role received mixed reactions. Some teachers at the elementary school welcomed the assistance; others resented what they regarded as an intrusion from a secondary school teacher. I had an additional problem of time, since I was still working at the secondary section as well as undertaking personal research for a postgraduate qualification. However, I used my position to investigate the problems related to learning English and I began to think that in order to solve these problems, we needed to improve the language curriculum. The first step would be to change the coursebooks in the elementary section.

Implementing the change

New books were ordered for inspection. Around this time the school was visited by the representative of a publishing company who briefed the senior teachers about a new literature-based reading programme developed by their company. The programme was originally designed for native speakers but was also suitable for EFL/ESL learners. The books looked interesting and the senior teachers and I agreed that a new approach to EFL teaching would be helpful, although challenging. The company assured us that they would provide training for the teachers if we decided to use the new books.

Following this meeting sample copies of the literature-based books arrived. The secondary school teachers were asked to examine the new books to advise whether they could be used in our school. Each teacher was given about two days to review her share of books. No guidelines were given to the teachers to follow when they evaluated the books. The elementary teachers were not asked to review any books although the change was going to take place in their section. A week after this, a meeting was held to discuss the results.

Evaluation of the change

In the section which follows, I will try to describe the events which took place during the introduction of the course materials. In describing the process of change I propose to follow the major factors suggested by Bolam (1976):

- the innovation: the change which is being implemented
- the innovating system: the user, the receiver, adopter or the client who is adopting an innovation
- the innovator system: the change agent who is implementing the change
- the innovation process

The innovation

The innovation was a new set of books which were proposed as a replacement for the existing EFL materials. There were fundamental differences between the new and the existing books. For example, the new materials were originally designed for native speakers, although support for second language learners was given for each lesson. The new books were based on children's literature and provided integrated activities for reading, speaking, listening and writing, with stories and attractive pictures. Shared reading was emphasized as a technique to provide the pupils with enjoyable language experiences as they were taught skills and strategies. The materials presented opportunities for the learners to hear and read authentic pieces of language.

The innovating system

The innovating system in this case consisted of the following:

- the teachers (users)
- the pupils (receivers)
- the school (client)

As the new books were different from the previous materials, the teachers would have to make adjustments to be able to use them effectively. Some conflict could be expected at this level as a result of the differences between the two programmes.

The pupils would also need to adapt to the new books. They could present a challenge to the learners because they were originally prepared for native speakers and contained authentic pieces of literature. The rationale behind the selection was that the demands made by these books would promote learning and have a positive effect on the overall achievement of the pupils.

The school administration would have to play a very important part by getting the new materials approved by the local educational authorities and by providing the resources to finance the new project.

The innovator system

The role of the change agent, as mentioned earlier, is believed to be crucial in the process of change. Gross et al. (1971) identifies the change agent's responsibilities to be the following:

1 to plan, support and monitor the innovation process
2 to clarify teachers' role definition
3 to provide access to training for the new role
4 to ensure that necessary materials are available
5 to modify organizational arrangements
6 to devise feedback mechanisms

In the process being described here, the change agents were myself and the other senior teachers. I suggested the change and strongly believed that new materials needed to be introduced, but was not totally in charge of the change, since I was not a senior teacher but an informal advisor. I also had my commitments to my work in the secondary section and my personal research. This meant a lack of clarity as to who was in charge of the innovation and no one effectively took on the responsibilities above.

The innovation process

A week after the arrival of the sample copies, a general meeting was held. All the teachers, both elementary and secondary, were asked to attend this meeting, chaired by one of the supervisors. Each teacher was asked to examine a few of the sample books which could be used at the levels she was teaching and to make comments about their suitability. The elementary teachers were not prepared for the task as they had not had a chance to examine the books prior to the meeting.

During the discussion which followed, the teachers expressed their concerns about the books they had examined. The following points were raised against adopting the new books:

1   The way language teaching was approached in the new language books was criticized because it was different from the traditional ways the teachers were used to in the EFL books. The teachers were concerned that the books did not identify which grammatical structures the learners had to master. The stories were not graded according to structural difficulty.

2   The new reading books were designed for native speakers and contained authentic pieces of literature which could be difficult to understand for the learners.

3   Some of the stories were not culturally appropriate.

4   There were new concepts in the books such as literature appreciation which would be hard for EFL pupils.

5   The books were expensive so the school would not agree to the change.

At the end of the meeting, it was decided that the new books were not suitable for our school and the meeting was adjourned by asking the teachers to keep looking for other more suitable materials.

This meeting seemed to mark the end of the innovation process. In the section that follows I shall give the reasons which caused the change to be rejected.

Reasons for failure

In this section I propose to analyse the reasons for the failure of the change by using Hurst's conditions for acceptance. Hurst (1983) identifies seven conditions which play a crucial part in the acceptance of a change:

1   communication

2   relevance or desirability

3   effectiveness or reliability

4 feasibility

5 efficiency

6 trialability

7 adaptability

Lack of communication between the participants and the management was apparent. The teachers were unaware of the discussions which took place between the supervisors and the publisher's representative. The teachers were not informed about the possibility of training sessions before they were to begin to use the books. No effort was made to explain to the teachers why these books were being considered in the first place. Moreover, the teachers were not allowed to get familiar with the books before they were asked to make decisions about using them.

From the comments made about the books, it is quite obvious that the teachers did not consider the new materials relevant to their situation as they were not specifically designed for non-native learners. The tendency to use traditional methods was quite strong among this group. It could have been predicted that using materials which promoted a different approach to language teaching would be unacceptable to a majority of the teachers. There was no attempt to help the teachers see the benefits of adopting these books.

The effectiveness and the reliability of the new materials seemed to be a major concern of the teachers. However, none of them had the opportunity to find out whether the new programme would prove to be effective if used with their students. They had to base their decisions on their intuitions instead. The proposed materials were based on different theories of language learning from those they were used to and the teachers did not have any previous experience of using such materials. The teachers involved in the decision-making process perceived a degree of risk from using these materials in their classrooms. Rather than take the risk, they rejected the books.

Another reason for the rejection of the change was probably that the teachers did not have the necessary guidance on what they were expected to do with the new materials. Adopting new books would require extra time and effort from the teachers and this was a further constraint. The teachers failed to see the advantages of using the new coursebooks because they were not given a chance to trial them before being asked to make a decision. If the books had been tried out prior to the decision-making stage, this would have helped the teachers to find out whether adopting the books would be beneficial. This could have reduced uncertainty and could have led to the adoption of the innovation.

The adaptability of the materials could have been discovered if they had been tried out with different groups of pupils. Necessary changes could have been made during the trial period. Problems which might have arisen from cultural differences could have been discussed and possible solutions sought with the co-operation of the teachers.

A second attempt

After the rejection of the change, I started to look for alternative course materials. The more I examined different course materials, however, the more I became convinced that a literature-based programme would provide the answers to the problems faced in our school. So I decided to try a second time to get these materials approved. The following account is a summary of the events which took place during the second attempt to change the course materials.

An in-service teacher training course was prepared for the elementary teachers. Two main issues were emphasized in the workshops held – language awareness for teachers, and teaching EFL/ESL to young learners. The rationale for organizing a training course was to familiarize the teachers with the new trends in EFL teaching, and to start an awareness in the teachers about how language actually works.

Teachers were observed to assess the effectiveness of the training programme, and to identify problems which could be used as input to further in-service training. Weekly meetings were arranged to discuss daily problems and ways to solve them. Teachers met in grade level groups to help focus on the specific problems of each level. In the meetings the focus was on issues like lesson planning, class management, and materials development. The representative of the books rejected paid our school another visit. This time a meeting was arranged for the teachers to talk to the representative.

During the following months we continued to meet every week with the first and second grade teachers. These meetings gave us a chance to focus on the problems caused by the existing EFL materials. We also had a chance to compare them with the new books. Soon we were using some of the material which appeared in the literature-based course to supplement the old books. We were also trying some of the techniques, such as shared reading, suggested in the new materials. The group meetings continued. These meetings served as an informal gathering to talk about the new books. I also had regular meetings with the principal throughout this time to explain the change to her and gain her support for the project.

The teachers' attitudes towards the new materials were beginning to change. The school was also in favour of the change. The teachers were beginning to see the advantages of the new books. However, there were still some concerns about the new programme. The teachers wanted to know how the change would affect them. They were worried about the number of books they were expected to use and the time they would have to spend to get the programme running. There were also some questions about their ability to meet the demands of the new programme. To address some of these concerns a meeting was held to explain to the teachers the components of the programme and how the distribution would be made among levels. During this meeting they were also informed of further training to help them learn how to use the new materials. The teachers were also assured of continuous support in weekly meetings during implementation. It was also decided that the new books would be introduced gradually, starting with the younger learners, to help both the teachers and the learners to get used to the change. The climate for change became more positive and the materials began to be introduced.

Conclusions

The analysis of the innovation process indicates that the seven conditions of acceptability proposed by Hurst were not met during the first attempt at change, and that attempts to address these problems at the second attempt proved more successful.

Loucks-Horsley and Stiegelbauer (1991) focus attention on the 'people response' to change. They believe that the process of change is a personal experience for each individual involved. They go on to explain that 'everyone approaching a change, initially implementing an innovation, or developing a skill in using an innovation will have certain perceptions, feelings, motivations, frustrations, and satisfactions about the innovation and the change process.' This individualized approach to change was clearly lacking in the first attempt. Improving communications between the people in charge of the change and the users is a first step in this approach. Change agents need to establish a good relationship with the teachers. Group meetings or personal interviews can be held to inform the teachers about the change, and to answer their questions and concerns about the innovation. Anxiety about problems that might arise as a result of adopting the change usually generates resistance. Users need continuous help and support during change. Providing the teachers with in-service training before and during the implementation of the change can prove to be effective (McLaughlin 1991). Such relatively simple strategies can make the difference between success and failure, as my brief account shows.

Kemale Pinar has worked in Turkey and Saudi Arabia as a teacher, trainer and administrator. She is now teaching Professional Communication Skills at Saint Mary's University, Halifax, Nova Scotia, Canada.

CALL innovation in the ELT curriculum

7

Simon Sergeant

Introduction

T
he complexity of Information Technology (IT) innovation and the speed of diffusion and technological advance seem to have left the English language teaching profession searching for ways of integrating IT usefully into the curriculum. While there seems to be little doubt of the potential of IT, it is difficult to specify the nature of the new learning opportunities. Papert (1987) and Perkins (1985) highlight the fact that there is much still to be discovered about the place of computer-assisted learning (CAL) in education, and this is still the case today. This article does not claim to produce answers, but I hope it will contribute to awareness of the problem. The aims of the article are:

- to examine the nature of CALL (computer-assisted language learning) innovation and its potential as a force for curricular change with examples drawn from my work in a language centre in Singapore;
- to investigate reasons for the shortfall between the potential of CALL and actual use, and discuss reasons why CALL opportunities are not taken;
- to indicate strategies by which a change agent may add value to a CALL facility.

Computers in commerce and industry are associated with higher efficiency. This assumption has been carried into the educational arena, and into language teaching in particular, with varying degrees of success. CALL as a discipline is establishing a research base after several years' local trial and error supported by anecdote. However, research is often carried out under ideal conditions which are only partially realizable within the constraints of everyday use. These local constraints are informed by attitudes of the major stakeholders in CALL: managers (usually non-users), CALL personnel (initial users), and teachers and students (end-users). Students, who are the recipients of CALL, are the least consulted during the decision-making process. They are also the ones who are most disadvantaged if CALL is not effectively implemented.

The full potential of integrating computers into the ELT curriculum has not yet been reached and their use is still limited. CALL is treated as a separate entity and bolted on to the existing curriculum. I will suggest in this article that due to the additional complexity of the computer medium compared with normal classroom activities, a high standard of teacher expertise is essential. Without this expertise not much useful learning takes place and CALL becomes a form of 'electronic baby-sitting'.

We have until now used 'change' as a super-ordinate term to include the notion of 'innovation' (see Introduction, piv). In this article, however, Sergeant distinguishes the two terms with respect to developments in computer-assisted language learning (CALL). He believes that the true benefits of CALL have rarely been realized. Normally, a CALL facility is set up and provides supplement-ary materials to an existing curriculum, as a peripheral 'bolt-on' activity. This use of CALL he defines as a 'change', in which a development has taken place (the introduction of a CALL resource) but the curriculum and the teaching and learning associated with it remain substantially the same. He regards this as a surface-level use of CALL. His appeal is to integrate CALL with the curriculum and use its power to create new ways of learning and teaching so that 'innovation', a re-thinking of the curric-ulum, can take place.

Background

CALL facilities have been available at the language centre for many years, starting with an exploratory project to investigate the pedagogic value of microcomputers in the ELT classroom. Since then, informal evaluation based on the observation of teachers and students using computers, positive comments in student questionnaires and informal discussions all suggest that on the whole, despite a small number of negative reactions from students, using computers to learn English can be enjoyable as well as educational.

CALL facilities have grown so that computers feature throughout our course structure. The main computer room houses a network of computers. Students usually work in pairs or groups of three. Timetabling is flexible. Slots are booked, usually a week in advance by teachers when they feel their class would most benefit. On a 100-hour full-time course, a student may spend ten hours using the computer. In terms of a quantitative evaluation, CALL in our centre has had an extremely high adoption rate. Over a ten-year period there have been between 300 000 and 350 000 half-hour lessons booked. The actual time students spend in front of a computer and the high degree of adoption by teaching staff is an important visible sign of success, especially as use is discretionary, but it conceals the important dimension of quality, which I shall return to later.

Teachers are trained in a number of ways. Each teacher has a short induction giving them a broad overview of CALL and how to use the most popular programs. The teacher is then supported by written information which offers more detailed help. A CALL co-ordinator (CC) is on hand to respond to questions as they arise, while more experienced teachers pass on their expertise. A special four-day training course, the CALL Teacher Education Course (CALLTEC), was also designed. CALLTEC aims to give teachers the theory and practical experience necessary for effective CALL use and materials development.

The fascination of the computer as machine

The introduction of computers into the culture of language learning is a complex change. When we think of CALL, the first impression is of the computer itself, apparently doing something sophisticated with students peering intently at the screen. Then we may reflect that the apparent sophistication is a stitched-together product of people and systems with their inherent flaws. Less obvious is the enthusiast working late behind the scenes trying to ensure that the stitches are not obvious and that the thing does not suddenly get out of control, by making the hardware, software, pedagogy, communications and infrastructure robust. We then need to add the reactions of the users and managers: enthusiastic, accepting, indifferent, cynical, nervous or rejecting. Finally, we step back and look at the whole picture, and reflect on how all these interacting elements constitute a new sub-culture of language learning.

It is clear that, together with a fascination for computers, many students rank acquisition of computing skills alongside the acquisition of English language as essential for survival in the modern world. Given the holding power of the computer, it is hardly surprising that we tend to foreground the computer and computer applications, when we should concentrate more on the interaction between the technology and the culture of learning. Papert (1987) calls this tendency technocentrism – making an object the centre of our attention. Technocentrism is endemic in CALL research and evaluation as well as in the way teachers, students and managers perceive computers in education. It often leads to the assumption that having provided the opportunity to use computers, learning happens by itself.

The ecology of CALL innovation

CALL, like any classroom innovation, takes place at many levels. 'The first important thing is that change is systemic, that is to say it takes place in an environment which consists of a number of interrelating systems.' (Kennedy 1988).

Kennedy employs a 'wheels within wheels' diagram in which classroom innovation forms the centre of the wheel, and institutional, educational, administrative, political and cultural levels form progressively outer circles. Chin and Benne (1976:33) discuss the problems of introducing new 'thing' technologies (for example, audio-visual devices, television, computers) into school situations:

> As attempts are made to introduce these new thing technologies into school situations, the change problem shifts to the human problems of dealing with the resistance, anxieties, threats to morale, conflicts, disrupted interpersonal communications and so on, which prospective changes in patterns of practice evoke in the people affected by the change.

Paisey (in White 1988:116) reminds us that

> ... it is people who inhabit an institution, and an organisation consists of networks of relationships between people acting and reacting on each other – thus organisations contain rational as well as non-rational elements ... Most crucially, an educational organisation is operated by the persons who are themselves the instruments of change. Without their willingness and participation, there will be no change.

These writers give some idea of the dynamics of introducing 'thing' technologies into interacting systems and subsystems, although they fall short of providing a detailed model of the curriculum in a state of flux.

Innovation or change?

White (1988) defines innovation as 'a deliberate effort, perceived as new and intended to bring about improvement'. It is distinguished from change, which is any difference between Time 1 and Time 2. Delano et al. (1994) define innovation more narrowly for the ESL context in terms of change, development, novelty and improvement. An innovation in a second language teaching programme is an informed change in an underlying philosophy of language teaching/learning, brought about by direct experience, research findings, or other means, resulting in an adaptation of pedagogic practices such that instruction is better able to promote language learning.

Kemmis et al. (1977) make a distinction between minimal and maximal curriculum innovation. Minimal innovation occurs when there is a change in the way a particular aspect of the syllabus is presented to students. The course will be altered to accommodate the new idea. Maximal innovation would be evident in a massive re-orientation of a course influenced by the CALL aspect of the course.

First order and second order innovation

Perkins (1985) sheds light on the way in which innovations are minimally adopted in education. He distinguishes between first and second order 'fingertip effects' of information processing technology. First order fingertip effects are the obvious differences an innovation makes, the immediate advantage put at one's fingertips, such as being able to converse with friends overseas (telecommunications), or easier typing (the word processor). Second order fingertip effects are the deeper repercussions of the innovation. The use of the word processor for instance puts a powerful tool at the fingertips of the L2 student of writing. The ability to create and manipulate text easily, to move, insert, copy or delete blocks before deciding how the completed document will appear, liberates the writer from linear constraints and from the chore of rewriting in long-hand.

The 'opportunities get taken' hypothesis (Perkins ibid) suggests optimistically that students will recognize the opportunity of large-scale editing. The deeper, second order effects involving a restructuring of the cognitive skills underlying the writing process will be 'soaked up' by assigning writing tasks on the word processor. In other words, the opportunity does the teaching by itself. However, Perkins claims, 'Most typically ... the opportunities are not taken.'

The nature of missed opportunities

Something will always be learned when a student engages in a CALL activity but this may not be even at Perkins' first order level. Opportunities for the deeper second level learning may also be missed. Consider the results of a survey of perceived program use among full-time students on a 100-hour intensive general English course. At the end of the course 200 students were asked which programs they had used and to estimate how many times they had used them. The results are shown in Figure 1.

One of Perkins' criteria for transfer of learning is a variety of wide-ranging practice. This is not occurring since almost 57 percent of perceived CALL use is accounted for by two programs: Storyboard[1] and Gapmaster[2]). Teachers are not exploring different programs. The popularity of Storyboard and Gapmaster may be accounted for by the ease of entering texts into the programs, or 'authoring'. To author Storyboard, teachers type in a text (author the program) and save it. The same applies to Gapmaster. Teachers place the words they want to blank out in square brackets. The texts used are usually extracts from student textbooks or grammar/vocabulary practice books.

---

[1] In Storyboard, students have to reassemble a text which has been deleted from the screen.
[2] Gapmaster is a form of cloze procedure, with students filling in missing words in a text.

Program	Student half-hours	%	Mode*
Storyboard	1266	38.3	Instructional/conjectural
Gapmaster	614	18.6	Instructional
Word processing	577	17.5	Emancipatory
Vocab Games	322	9.8	Instructional
Testmaster	150	4.5	Instructional
Grammar Games	116	3.5	Instructional
Clarity Grammar	94	2.8	Instructional
Pinpoint	49	1.5	Instructional/ conjectural
Fast Food	35	1.1	Revelatory
Wordstore	34	1.0	Instructional
FCE Exercises	22	0.7	Instructional
Matchmaster	13	0.4	Instructional
London Adventure	10	0.3	Revelatory

*Instructional: learners recall what has been taught
Revelatory: learners take part in a relatively structured learning situation, eg a simulation
Conjectural: learners engage in tasks with open-ended, unpredictable solutions
Emancipatory: learners engage in authentic, real activities

Figure 1: Perceived program use

Another way of getting closer to the nature of missed opportunities is to relate the level of actual program use to types of learning generated by CALL. Kemmis et al. (1977) distinguish five learning styles for CAL, which Phillips (1985) uses to map the types of learning naturally arising from a particular program type. These are recognition, recall, comprehension, experimental and constructive understanding. In the first style, the student is required merely to recognize previously presented language forms. In the second, the student is required to reproduce previously acquired knowledge. Neither recognition nor recall involve the active construction of new knowledge. The third type, comprehension, involves a more active role and entails the ability to operate on a body of content and transform it in some way. Experimental learning may involve the active exploration of a simulation. Language production is less constrained by on-screen text. Constructive understanding involves using the computer as a tool to discover new language.

The most common use of Storyboard is for students to retrieve a text which they have previously encountered in their textbook. Storyboard contains a 'cheat' feature which means that at any time a student may see the entire text again without a penalty. The same applies to individual words. Both these strategies are used by students to reduce learning load. Though teachers intend this activity to improve comprehension, the type of learning arising from this activity is usually at the level of recognition or recall. Copying a text verbatim may help students to remember words or syntactic structures, spelling may improve, and it is probably more fun than copying a text using pen and paper.

If they work on a Storyboard activity collaboratively, students may learn something from the language they use to complete the text, though research on the nature of talk generated in front of CALL programs summarized by Nicholls (1992) and Nicholls' own research on Storyboard in particular suggest that conversational spin-off is limited. The discourse produced is impoverished in terms of lexical and syntactic variety, with many single word utterances and repetitions of screen text, and it is of limited pedagogical value.

Gapmaster is most frequently used in the drill-and-practice mode. An exercise from a grammar textbook is typed in, for instance to practise question tags. The outcome is fixed and non-negotiable. The facility of the program to accept more than one correct answer requires more effort by a teacher to author the alternatives (enter the text required) and is often not used. The off-screen interaction is limited and the learning is at the level of recognition or recall.

The problem of opportunities for learning not being taken deepens when the mode of the CALL experience is considered (Figure 1). CALL in the instructional mode accounts for 81 percent of total use, whereas CALL in the revelatory mode accounts for 1.4 percent. Word processing accounts for the total use of CALL in the emancipatory mode at 17.5 percent. CALL in the instructional mode involves no negotiation of outcome. The aim of activities is for the student to produce text which has been pre-determined before the activity began. They involve the manipulation of language in ways which do not involve any exchange of meaning. Transformation exercises and controlled pattern practice are activities which involve the production of language but not the use of language (Willis 1990). This approach is therefore at odds with current communicative language teaching methodology which asserts that people learn a language best by using the language to achieve real meanings and outcomes. Underwood (1984) comments that CALL in this mode tries to simulate what the teacher does in the classroom – to be exact, the least interesting things. It tends to be authoritarian, evaluative and overly structured. The shortfall between the potential learning opportunities that could be realized and the reality of the way programs are frequently underused is obvious.

Summary of the problem

Teachers with a low level of CALL expertise are less likely to be aware of the range of opportunities offered by authoring and using well designed CALL activities, though some novices make up for this by being enthusiastic and creative because they do not have preconceived ideas. During a four-hour lesson, migrating to the computer room is a welcome change of scene which tends to give the teacher and students a break from each other. Once a task has been set, the teacher can take a more passive role, offering guidance only when required, sometimes not at all. Teachers take a technocentric viewpoint and assume that the minimal task imposed by the program, whether gap filling, test reconstruction, or interacting at a basic level with a simulation, constitutes a worthwhile task.

Each time teachers use a new CALL activity, it represents a micro-innovation. Teachers will usually make a cost/benefit calculation based on how much benefit their classes will receive from half an hour in front of the computer offset against the amount of effort and risk involved. The effort teachers need to put into learning a new program and training their students to take part in an activity will be calculated. The risk of failure is an important part of the calculation, based on perception of the reliability of the hardware and the complexity of the program. The more complex a program is, the more a teacher will fear the failure of the activity due to someone pressing the wrong key or entering part of the program that the teacher has not yet discovered. A number of personal failures, for example with word processing, may discourage a teacher from using valuable activities, and staffroom anecdotes about such experiences will discourage other teachers. As a consequence, the safer, less complex activities tend to be favoured by the majority.

Certain factors militate against the use of more time-consuming integrated activities such as simulations, which involve the class and the teacher in learning how to use a program that has less repeat value than a text reconstruction activity. This type of program involves more preparation and time in terms of pre-CALL and post-CALL activities in the classroom. There is the need to complete the textbook material prescribed for the lesson, which is especially the case where classes are shared by more than one teacher, so 'extra' activities, which are less obviously related to course content, may be less used. There is, therefore, a danger of over-using a small number of programs and requiring students to use the same program (with different texts) repeatedly.

A similar cost/benefit calculation applies to the creation of materials. Certain programs such as Storyboard are easy to author (enter text) and highly productive in terms of the ratio of authoring time and effort to the amount of student use. Storyboard has a consistent history of almost 100 percent reliable use, so there are few lost lessons. Under conditions of teacher ownership, materials are written into courses using these easily mastered packages which produce as much student 'busyness' as possible for the least effort in materials writing or lesson preparation.

Most materials exist only as texts. They are supplementary to the textbook materials. They are easily authored materials written into courses, so that a particular unit in a textbook may be supplemented with a text reconstruction activity, a vocabulary activity and/or a gap-filling activity. They are written into the teacher's notes, and become institutionalized, fixed supplementary elements for a particular course. The syllabus then becomes resistant to more integrated activities in emancipatory or revelatory modes, such as word processing or simulations. At this stage it is difficult to alter the materials or introduce a wider variety of programs.

The preponderance of CALL materials in the instructional mode (see Figure 1) reflects the nature of the wider syllabus, primarily derived from textbooks with a structural/functional ordering of items. In the wider syllabus these structures and functions are supplemented with further materials of the same nature. A number of communicative activities are also available, but are considered secondary to the process of teaching the subject matter of the syllabus. This is also reflected in the balance of CALL materials. The prevalence of the supplementary use of CALL tends to define the normal level of CALL use, which is the typical level of adoption of the majority of teachers.

CALL implementation strategies

CALL expertise is a complex skill which can be acquired by various means. In an ideal situation, the CC (CALL co-ordinator) gains expertise by studying the field intensively, by talking to other practitioners and by everyday observation and practice. A selection of these skills are simplified and transferred to teachers through in-service training in various forms and through dealing with everyday problems and queries. A similar selection, simplification and transfer of skills takes place between teacher and students.

The CC, in his/her efforts to ensure effective CALL lessons, is in the position of co-ordinating the interaction of two highly complex systems: networked computers and the staff within the organization (see Appendix on p85). To ensure adoption, the CC can therefore work at the 'thing' level or at the 'person' level. Working at the 'thing' level leads to ease of access for all users: students, teachers and materials writers. Working at the 'person' level involves creating and maintaining a flow of information between all stakeholders within the institution, both users (students and teachers) and non-users (managers, technical staff, administrative staff – see Appendix).

On a day-to-day basis, the CC makes decisions about the most effective line of work, whether to focus activity from the bottom-up of the system (eg materials development, writing clear instructions/documentation) or from the top-down (eg teacher training, maintaining the goodwill of the management). Everyday priorities usually involve the bottom-up approach, dealing with problems as they arise, working under the assumption that if things are running smoothly, the goodwill of the management is assured. Improvements made to the system, materials and instructions are permanent, whereas training and retraining is a constant requirement for new staff or for those requiring updating. Most of the time it is more profitable to focus on permanent improvements. For example, something can be made easier for teachers to use, perhaps simplifying a procedure by a single key press, or writing clearer instructions. If this is multiplied by 40 staff or 2000 student users, it means that far less training is required.

The full implementation of CALL is a lengthy process. Five years were needed in our centre for the institutionalization of a minimal level of CALL: to set up system structures, to source software, to provide instructions to teachers, to author high quality materials and weave them into the structure of courses. Eight years were required before our centre achieved the standard of implementation and expertise required to generate a teacher training course such as CALLTEC.

Summary of value-adding activities

The summary in the Appendix to this article illustrates the ways in which a teacher with responsibility for CALL may add value to a CALL facility by working with managers, teachers and students either at the 'thing' (system) level or at the 'person' level.

Where only a small amount of non-teaching time is made available, the main focus of activity tends to shift away from teacher training to other considerations which, while they are more mundane, are the sine qua non of CALL: trouble shooting, software acquisition and installation, timetabling, maintenance of materials (printing, cataloguing, deletion, file backup) and therefore the level of use decreases in scope and quality. The provision of more time allows the CC to focus on value-adding activities which are less concerned with the day-to-day running of the facility such as teacher training, developing interesting materials, evaluation and self-education.

Conclusion

With insufficient management, the level of CALL use is likely to decline. The change agent, in this case the CALL co-ordinator (CC), is central to the process of ensuring that CALL operates smoothly. The CC deals with practical problems, and ensures that the innovation is at least minimally implemented. The CC can minimize problems faced by users of CALL by 'adding value' to the system at various levels. On a larger scale, the actions of the CC are pivotal to the process of significant curriculum change. These actions are responsible for facilitating conscious learning opportunities by ensuring that CALL learning exists, and that managers, teachers and students recognize these opportunities and take them.

To create and maintain the CALL facility in good working order requires a professional change agent: the CALL co-ordinator (CC) or a team of professionals with a high degree of expertise in CALL. They can interpret CALL use in terms of current methodology, define, create and maintain high quality learning structures and communicate their potentials to managers and users simply and effectively. The CC is responsible for the creation and maintenance of a student learning niche within the curriculum. Ideally, therefore, the expertise of the CC as change agent should include at least a rudimentary appreciation of how CALL is embedded in the curriculum and how to manage the innovation.

In this article, I have explored the nature of day-to-day CALL value-adding activity within the context of the CALL facility where I work. I put forward possible strategies for dealing with problems arising from the institutionalization of a minimal level of CALL use. The resolution of these problems is seen as a precondition for maximal benefit to the ELT curriculum.

Appendix

Value-adding activities

1 Working with non-users (managers)

Influencing
Influencing the private evaluation of CALL by managers, on the level of finance and hardware/software.

Technical matters
Reassuring managers that the technical performance of the system is robust and reliable.

Materials development
Encouraging managers to have an active interest and investment in materials development for CALL.

Teacher training
Encouraging the management to initiate and develop various forms of teacher training.

Communications
Improving the information flow between CALL personnel and managers.

Evaluation
Evaluation by managers of CALL on the level of consumer satisfaction, observable organizational change and flow of communication.

2 Working with users (teachers and students)

Working at the system level
Designing and programming the system to make it reliable and transparent to use, and identifying the need for new hardware.

Software evaluation and acquisition
Initiating the purchase or design of new software and submitting it to materials writers for evaluation.

Guiding CALL use
Administering the timetable. Writing instructions and manuals to support CALL use. Cataloguing and publishing materials in a form that teachers find useful when planning lessons.

Materials development
Writing materials and model lessons and supporting teachers who are authoring courseware.

Teacher training
Initiating and developing teacher training, ranging from presentations and workshops to responding to the day-to-day questions of individual teachers. Training may be either in the use of existing activities or in the creation of materials.

Evaluation
Evaluating the level of CALL use and the contribution CALL can make to different courses.

Influencing
Changing the way teachers think about CALL. This level is the private domain of the teacher, concerned with how teachers relate to CALL and the way CALL is integrated into a lesson at the planning stage.

Simon Sergeant is working at the British Council in Singapore. His interests are in CALL and innovation management.

8 Introducing technology in language teaching: video and computers

Patricio Bracamonte

Introduction

Bracamonte, like Sergeant in the previous article, looks at the difficulties of introducing technology change and emphasizes the importance of the interaction between the technology and the people using it. He looks at two technologies in his case study, based in an institute in Chile: video and computers. He shows how the teachers he was working with reacted differently to the two technologies, prompting a different way of introducing each technology to the users.

Technology is part of our lives. The economic–technological competition that characterizes the world forces its uses in educational contexts of all sorts. The supposed failure of conventional teaching methods to achieve better results in students' performance has focused educational specialists' attention on new, more modern methods to improve teaching and to bridge the gap between the 'school culture' and the 'real world'. Video and computers have become useful tools in this modern teaching/learning process and both belong to the world our students live in. The widespread use of technology in business, banking and commerce has also brought a lowering of prices, making technology more easily accessible to educational and training centres.

This article describes the attempts to implement the use of video and computers at the ELT institute where I work in Santiago, Chile. Although this case study is a subjective judgement of a specific situation, it is my hope that the results of the experience can be of some use to others who are planning to introduce technology in their own teaching/learning contexts.

Changes

There are different types of educational changes, ranging from the use of blackboard and chalk to the use of whiteboard and marker, or the use of a dictionary to that of an electronic computer database. People react in different ways to change, although 'the most common reaction to change is resistance' (Hutchinson 1991:8) and the more unfamiliar the change, the more resistance it generates.

The introduction of technology – video and computers – brings not only changes in the organization of the school, study centre or university (complex timetables, technicians, extra rooms, software expenditure) but also 'changes in terms of behaviour (and the attitudes and values that underline that behaviour) required of the people involved in order to accommodate themselves to the actual innovation' (ibid:6). This means changes in teachers' attitudes in the classroom towards adopting and adapting new methodologies to suit not only their needs but also their students' needs.

These two types of changes – organizational and behavioural – may, if successful, contribute to social change. In the case of video and computers, the aim is to develop more autonomous, creative and self-confident learners who can develop their cognitive abilities and put them to work in the real world.

The background

The institute has three branches in Santiago which offer general English courses for children, teenagers and adults, and is the examination centre for Cambridge Exams, including the TEFL Diploma. There is an ESP department which runs company courses and which also offers courses in Spanish as a foreign language. A teacher training college at the institute awards TEFL degrees after four years of full-time study.

Video implementation

There were two facts that allowed the almost immediate use of video and its integration with classroom work. An ESP course was being planned for a group at the Chilean Foreign Ministry who wanted their course to be 'modern' and 'different'; and the institute was used as a testing centre for BBC video material later published as 'Television English', so video material was provided free of cost by the BBC.

I propose now to examine the introduction of this video technology in the light of Rogers and Shoemaker's (1971:22) outline of the characteristics of innovation as perceived by receivers, in this case teachers and students.

1 Relative advantage
This is measured not in economic terms, but in terms of social prestige, convenience and satisfaction. Teachers quickly realized the need to adopt video because it raised the levels of motivation in their students and it elevated their status as professionals able to use technology. This was a cause of satisfaction for them and for their students. In addition, preparation for lessons using video was not significantly different from that for conventional lessons (a cost-effectiveness factor).

2 Compatibility
This is defined as the degree to which an innovation is perceived as being consistent with the existing values, past experience and needs of the receivers. Video proved to be an ideal tool to foster interaction among students, and in many cases it was easy to relate teaching points or topics to the software available.

3 Observability
This is the degree to which the results of the innovation are visible to others. In this case teachers' and students' comments inside and outside the institution proved influential, plus institutional support for software acquisition, in-service training seminars and subscriptions to journals. Above all, teachers were themselves convinced that this was a useful, motivating and practical tool which could enhance the teaching/learning process.

4 Complexity

This is the degree to which innovations may be understood and implemented. Because of its similarity with TV and the normal cassette recorder, it did not take teachers long to learn how to operate videos. Seminars, training courses and sample lessons were running periodically to make teachers feel confident in the handling of the new technology. Teachers were encouraged to turn to their own students for help in the event of any technical problems.

5 Trialability

This is the degree to which an innovation may be experimented with. Teachers were always encouraged to use video, never forced to use it. Those who were reluctant to use it and did so only after a long time were influenced by:

a) their own colleagues who recommended its use, and who prepared/lent materials or provided pedagogical advice and moral support;

b) their own students who in previous sessions had had lessons in which video had been used successfully.

After a stage of familiarization of about a year and a half in which training sessions and seminars took place, it was suggested that adolescent and adult courses at the institute would be scheduled for two video sessions per term (each term consisted of 33 teaching hours). One of these sessions would be prepared and taught by a demonstrator (the teacher in charge of video – myself), using appropriate video materials related to the teaching point being dealt with in class, with the class teacher as an observer. The second class would be taught by the class teacher who, if required, could have prior meetings with the demonstrator in order to get help either in the handling of the equipment or for anything pedagogical. The scheme was implemented with highly successful results, so much so that it was the teachers who suggested the system of timetabled sessions should continue the following term.

Today the use of video has become a normal feature of the language classroom at the institute and seminars and workshops are run to introduce new materials and to prepare and adapt activities and worksheets for them. Although there are no formal statistics on the frequency of use of this technology, all full-time teachers and over 60 percent of the part-time teachers use video at least once a term with all their classes.

Computer implementation

The institute in Santiago took delivery of a microcomputer and a small selection of software. Three members of staff began experimenting with the computer and shared their findings among themselves and with other colleagues, and attended a training course.

Nine more computers were bought and a similar scheme to the one used to introduce video was implemented. Unfortunately, despite staff training courses, workshops and seminars as well as timetable scheduling, teachers showed reluctance to use CALL with their students.

The reasons for this failure, using Rogers and Shoemaker's model once more, would seem to be the following:

1 Relative advantage
In terms of convenience and satisfaction computers scored negatively, frightened teachers, and as a result teachers were reluctant to use CALL.

2 Compatibility
Teachers had no past experience in the use of the technology and although they recognized it was a motivating tool, they felt it was a field for specialists.

3 Observability
The number of classes with computers were not enough to spread their use, so the results of the innovation were not visible to other teachers and students.

4 Complexity
a) The computer is a highly interactive tool but one to which teachers may sometimes assign a 'God function' (Hurst 1983:10). Teachers are nervous of a machine that can replace them or may have the power to control what occurs in the classroom.

b) The skills required to operate the machine are more complex.

c) Teachers are expected to operate and solve problems at two levels at the same time:

   i) Technical level: If technical problems arise, eg the program does not load, students press the wrong keys, a program crashes, the teacher is expected to solve the problem.

   ii) Pedagogical level: The teacher must still answer language questions, make the class interact, conduct activities, guide, correct, reward and so on.

d) Materials have too many different sub-menus, and programs are difficult to remember and locate.

e) There is usually too much software and this software is presented to teachers at the same time.

f) There are fewer specialists among teachers.

g) Teachers have a humanistic, rather than a scientific background.

5 Trialability
Although teachers were encouraged to use CALL, their use was led by the more experienced teachers so they were never confident enough to use computers on their own.

People will often follow the principle of 'inertia', that is, it is easier to do what you are familiar with, to be on the safe side, than try out something new. This familiarity makes them feel relaxed and at ease. Even if there is goodwill in support of the innovation, the change agent still has to overcome the difficulties of changing the awareness of those with whom he/she works so that they come to share the assumption that the changes will be of benefit to all.

Real changes

The institute recognized the need to implement CALL, despite the initial failure, and a group became involved in the process at two levels: with teachers and with students. It was agreed that changes would be implemented within a set period of time. Six teachers, two from each branch of the institute, were invited to take part in a Special Interest Group which would meet for two hours every week. It was agreed with the director that at least one of these hours would either be paid as overtime or would become part of the teachers' paid timetable. Lunch would also be paid for by the institute. During these sessions teachers were:

- trained in the use of the hardware;
- familiarized with the existing software;
- encouraged to integrate CALL with their usual classroom work;
- invited to share their knowledge and experience with their colleagues.

Working on the principle that knowledge of an innovation can generate motivation, the work of this Special Interest Group continued and expanded for two years until it covered the areas shown in the chart below:

CALL interest group		
In-service training/evaluation for institute teachers	Classroom research	Materials/ software preparation

In addition, a course on Computers in Education and TEFL was planned, run and evaluated. It was a 60-hour course for trainees at the teacher training college and it consisted of:

- classroom work;
- field work: visits to schools where computers were used in order to get information about hardware and software; visits to shops where hardware and software were sold;
- workshops: training on hardware, software, word processing.

The course was run by a university lecturer in Information Technology and myself. Seven trainees from the teacher training college who had successfully completed the course were employed by the institute as part-time assistants to carry out the tasks shown in the chart below:

CALL assistants			
Help institute teachers operate computers	Run self-access centre, tutorial programmes and word processors	Peer training (word processing)	Help college teachers

More PCs were bought and a CALL laboratory was set up at the institute. Programs for Spanish courses were prepared by the CALL Interest Group in co-ordination with the Spanish teachers and a plan for the use of concordancing programs has been implemented. So CALL has spread and it is hoped that resistance from the teachers is getting less, especially as more teachers get involved in the use of computers, since 'people fear isolation from their groups and so will resist straying too far from the group norm' (Hutchinson 1991:8).

Conclusions

1   When implementing technology in ELT it is important to be aware that technological tools have different characteristics and cannot be treated in the same way.

2   A useful way of introducing changes which provoke resistance is by means of a system made up of integrated elements to get the task done. The case study presented here is a clear example of the use of this system.

3   Technology is no longer part of the future and teachers should make an effort to become 'literate' in its use and to incorporate it into the teaching/learning process.

Patricio Bracamonte works at the British Institute in Santiago, Chile. His main interests are teacher training and computer-assisted language learning.

3 Classroom change

We saw in Section 1 examples of national change and the effects in the classroom of top-down change. The case studies in Section 2 also described top-down change but within institutions where someone was responsible for implementing the change and acting as an intermediary between management and teachers, and where there was more opportunity for feedback on the part of teachers. In Section 3 we continue the theme of individuals responsible for implementing change but now move closer to the classroom and the changes that take place within it. We look at the changes that practising teachers can implement in their own classrooms. This form of change is perhaps more familiar to readers as one of the many terms which characterize teacher-initiated enquiry like action learning or action research (Wallace 1998).

Such change can take many forms and Roberts' case study is an illustration of one of them. She wished to get a group of teachers together in her college to work on teacher-initiated research. She wanted to see whether, by developing collaborative activity, the group could overcome feelings of isolation, develop self-confidence, and bridge gaps between theory and practice. Roberts was the initiator of the activity and was herself writing up her experiences for her own research purposes, so there were two levels of reflection operating: reflection by the individuals in the group, and by Roberts herself. The article is a description of the process and also evaluates some of the advantages and disadvantages of teacher-initiated enquiry.

Collaboration worked to some extent, but teachers found it difficult to understand and listen to one another's problems. Their confidence grew, but teachers were sometimes unwilling to talk about problems or change their teaching, and reluctant to look at the theory behind what they were doing. This may of course have been due to the nature of the experiment and the individual characteristics of those participating. The process did appear to highlight a continuum from those teachers who act intuitively to those who reflect and try to seek reasons why a practice works or not.

Roberts feels she has learned more about the skills of a change agent and sets out a number of points for good practice, some of which reinforce what we have already considered in the previous chapters. These include trying to set the action research within the educational goals of the institution; ensuring support from and communication with the top; maximizing a sense of ownership in those taking part; and considering ways in which a reflective approach may be encouraged.

One effect of classroom-based research which Roberts found was that it led teachers to consult and obtain feedback from their students, which they found valuable. We have not closely considered the role of the learner, the ultimate implementer of change, in this volume but clearly the learner is part of the system of change and has the power to facilitate or obstruct it. The final case study by Pollari draws attention to the role of the learner in change and how important it is for a change agent to gather feedback on classroom change from those it most intimately affects. Pollari describes the shift from a teacher-centred to a learner-centred curriculum which is taking place in Finland. Against this background, she then reports an experiment in the development of student portfolios which she undertook in a secondary school together with three English language teachers from the school. This was an action research project similar to that described by Roberts, with a facilitator, Pollari, and three teachers investigating a learning approach which put new demands on themselves and their students. In this case, the research appears to have been a success, probably because the conditions that Roberts describes as necessary were operating. What both articles show is the importance of consulting learners about the innovation and obtaining feedback from them.

Key points

- Teacher enquiry is one way of enabling teachers to bring about change in their own classrooms, as well as helping them understand changes that have been imposed from outside the classroom.
- One type of enquiry can be carried out by small groups with a facilitator.
- Teacher enquiry encourages action with evaluation.
- Teacher enquiry will be successful only if certain conditions are fulfilled (eg support from above; sense of ownership).
- Classroom research encourages teachers to gain feedback from their students which therefore brings learners into the innovation process as participants.
- Teachers will respond differently to teacher enquiry – teachers cannot be forced to undertake research unwillingly.
- Teacher enquiry may complement and strengthen top-down change; it is unlikely to lead to significant bottom-up change outside the institution in which it is based.

Conclusion

The case studies in this collection have taken us from national change through to classroom change, and individuals have described the changes they have been a part of. Each individual has been learning how to implement change and, lacking training in change management, has been forced to learn as a part of the job. Our intention is that some of what they have learned may be passed on to those who read this book so that if readers have or take on similar change agent roles, they will be able to benefit from the ideas presented.

9 Evaluating teacher-initiated research: description of a pilot study

Rachael Roberts

Introduction

This article describes and evaluates an exploratory programme of teacher-initiated research which was undertaken over a ten-week period. A brief description of the context and the actual process of the programme will be followed by the main focus of the article – the perceived outcomes of the process and the insights gained by myself and my colleagues involved in the research.

The context

The EFL department in which I worked was in a college of further education in the UK. The students were both full-time and part-time, both native speakers and non-native speakers. Some of this latter group were studying subjects other than English and required English language support; some were living in the area temporarily and working as au pairs, and some were more properly termed ESL students, resident in the country but still requiring language assistance. The department was staffed by two full-time lecturers/administrators and eleven part-time lecturers. The atmosphere was generally supportive and comfortable, but because most of the teachers only came in for short periods of time to teach, there was little communication between many of the teachers on a regular basis. As a result there were limited opportunities for teachers to find out what colleagues were doing in their classrooms and to ask anyone for help and advice. The teachers felt undertrained and were not confident about their abilities. They would have liked more in-service training but, as simply another part-time lecturer, I was not in a position to provide a teacher training course as such. Instead, I wanted to discover whether, and to what extent, teacher-initiated research might help to improve these teachers' professional situation.

In attempting this I had three main objectives:

1 To combat the feelings of isolation (both personal and professional) teachers might be feeling and develop a collaborative and supportive network.
2 To develop teachers' confidence in their own capacities to empower themselves: building self-esteem and autonomy.

Most of the case studies in this volume deal with the problems that 'insiders' have in implementing change. 'Insiders' work in the institution in which the change is taking place and have not been recruited from outside to manage the change. In some cases their position in the organization gives them formal authority over those implementing the change (Doyle, Bracamonte). In this evaluation of an action research project by Roberts, the insiders are co-participants in the change. Their informal influence as facilitators of a collaborative group is given to them voluntarily by members of the group and can be withdrawn at any time. An interesting aspect of this case study is the light it throws on the thoughts and actions of individual teachers and how they react differently to action research. A simple evaluation such as this can provide such insights which in turn become part of the learning process of the change agent.

3   To provide for a bridging between theory and practice: lacking a great deal of in-service training, teachers felt the need for input but often failed to see the relevance of books and articles or one-off seminars to their own situation.

This pilot study could not have the effects of a long-term project but I hoped that the insights gained could prove useful in making long-term future changes in this context and to other teacher trainers setting up similar projects. I wanted to exploit my position as a member of the institution, with an insider perspective, to take a genuine part in the classroom research while simultaneously acting as an observer of the process.

Describing the process

The beginning

A starting point for any teacher-initiated research is the identification of a shared concern amongst the participants – a joint problem which can be consensually addressed. Four colleagues felt able to commit themselves to the project, and after some discussion the teaching of the skill of writing was identified as an area of common concern. Having done some preliminary reading and thinking about the area, we arranged our first group meetings. I had originally thought of all four teachers collaborating together but it only proved possible to meet in two pairs, with me present at each meeting. We agreed that follow-up meetings would be held two or three weeks later in order to discuss issues and make any modifications to the original plan of action, to be followed by final meetings to evaluate progress and make plans for the future.

In conjunction with these meetings I also asked participants to keep a diary. As McDonough (1994) points out, diary keeping is a natural choice of tool for the teacher as researcher paradigm, providing a means 'for teachers to formulate context specific issues out of the reality of their classroom.' Bailey (1990) cites a study by Butler-Wall (1979:6), who notes that keeping a diary helped her 'to sort out recurring issues, important questions, and points to keep an eye on in the future.' Writing a diary can thus be viewed like discussion, as a discovery process – a way to generate and explore ideas, make connections, argue, question and in this way conduct an internal dialogue. I also intended to keep my own diary recording my day-to-day thoughts and changing perspective on the project as a whole.

Setting the agenda with the first group

I would now like to briefly summarize some of the themes raised and actions taken by the participants over the period of the project. The first meeting to be held was with the two teachers I shall call Claire and Sarah. There was a great deal of discussion about different aspects of writing. Some recurring themes were the lack of enthusiasm for writing among the students and the importance of having a reason to write. We also felt that students tended not to take responsibility for their own writing. We looked particularly at how we might deal with correction. The following plan of action was decided upon.

1 Talk to students about writing, finding out more about their attitudes, likes and dislikes, problems.

2 Use a correction code.

3 Put aside the first ten minutes for correction.

4 Ask students to write on alternate lines, in order to facilitate comments and correction, including self-correction.

5 Ask students to self-monitor, annotating with queries as they write (as suggested by Charles 1990).

Claire found a student questionnaire in Hedge (1988), entitled 'What do you think about your writing?', which we implemented. The feedback from this was discussed in our second meeting. It seemed that students were keen on improving the formal aspects of writing and generally enthusiastic about the use of the correction code and, theoretically at least, willing to take more responsibility. Claire was pleased with the results, commenting that, 'I think it pays off, I find that it does make them think.' However, as she added, '... if I had ten or twelve students doing it each time I wouldn't fit it into fifteen minutes.' In her diary, Claire concluded: 'I don't think I have satisfactorily resolved the problem of correction and double correction within the allotted timespan, (however) I think that the correction code has been a good thing on the whole and has led to more critical awareness on the part of the student.'

At the same second meeting, Sarah felt that perhaps the use of a correction code was not so suitable for her particular group of students. A student suggestion had been for them to correct their own work at home, but Sarah felt a more realistic option would be to use the last fifteen minutes of the class time for self-correction and so it was decided to adopt this plan. Although Sarah retained reservations about the use of a correction code for her group of students, she did feel that, overall, it had been a useful experience in focusing both her and her students on certain important issues.

Setting the agenda with the second group

The second group, with the participants I shall refer to as Joanne and Teresa, identified the antipathy to writing the students sometimes had as an important area to focus on. We felt that they needed more motivation and a reason to write. Project work seemed to provide a possible solution and we discussed the possibility of learners collaborating on a type of alternative students' handbook for next year's students. This would be suitable for all levels and could involve working in groups and, with publication as an end, focusing on the process of planning, drafting, writing and editing.

The plan of action decided upon was to:

1 talk to students about writing, for the reasons mentioned above;

2 focus on the process of writing;

3 suggest the idea of a student handbook as a possible motivation;

4 encourage students to see teachers as a resource rather than a guide;

5 encourage peer correction;

6 break tasks down into manageable sizes and give more praise and encouragement.

At the next meeting we shared feedback. Joanne felt that a lot had been gained from discussing the issues with her students. In her diary she had described the reactions of one of the students: 'Sometimes she just feels that nothing happens. She gets the writing back with corrections and that's it. I think she would wish to share it more, and see examples of other ways of doing it.'

Teresa's students were at a more elementary level and she had obviously found it more difficult to elicit their attitudes and opinions. She had also come to the conclusion that it would be difficult for them to contribute to the proposed handbook, saying at the feedback discussion: 'Well, I just feel my elementary students, they write so little and what we're doing, making up sentences and things, I just felt that this was a little way beyond them when we came to do it.' She felt that they had a generally negative attitude towards writing, so we discussed possible ways of encouraging students to write at that level. It was decided that she would try encouraging the students to start a learner diary, in which they could record what they had learned, problems and achievements. It was felt that this might have the double purpose of both encouraging writing and encouraging reflection on their own part in the learning process.

Joanne and I decided to continue working on the handbook project. The students involved in this project did eventually produce some excellent work for the handbook, and we felt that this had been largely as a result of the increased motivation they felt in producing something relevant and which needed to be well written. Joanne also felt that the project had affected her practice in that it had 'made me look at writing in a much more varied way and to see it more from the students' point of view.'

However, Teresa had finally decided against the idea of a learner diary, explaining that she 'felt it was something they couldn't really handle effectively'. She had a group of students who were partly EFL and partly ESL and felt that the ESL students might not have the educational background to be sufficiently reflective. On the whole, it had not been an entirely successful experience for Teresa. It seemed clear that she had, from the outset, been looking for something different from the project:

> No, I've got to admit that I don't think it was particularly useful to me, in that I haven't got a lot of ideas out of it for myself ... for actual sort of tips and techniques. I haven't got that much from it, but then that's perhaps not what it was all about to start with – was it?

Evaluating the outcomes

Having related briefly something of the process of the project, I would now like to consider how far the project might be considered to have been successful. What might the participants have actually gained from the experience and to what extent could the guiding aims of the project be said to have been achieved? Had working together on a teacher-initiated research project been able to, or shown the potential to significantly improve the situation of the participants? If not, what factors might this be due to?

1 How far had the project been able to combat the feelings of isolation teachers might be feeling and to develop a collaborative and supportive network?

This was the aim in which, superficially at least, the project was most evidently successful. All the teachers involved pointed out how pleased they had been to have been able to spend time talking about teaching. Although the atmosphere within the college was open and co-operative there was normally little chance to work together or see each other teach. Participants in the project frequently became so involved in discussion that meetings tabled to last no more than one hour went on for two, leading me to conclude that the teachers did indeed, as Teresa said, value an opportunity to 'share things with people of like mind and in the profession you are.' That said, it is, however, doubtful how much they discovered, or even wanted to know, about each other's situations. I asked Claire about this:

> I never really got to know what anybody else was doing. I think Sarah thought it was a good idea from the point of view of making them aware of their mistakes, but I don't really know what she thought about the other things, whether she did the other things, I don't know.

In fact the participants did describe what they had been doing and the make-up of their classes in some detail. That participants did not recognize this may have been due to a perceived lack of relevance to their own immediate needs, especially considering the limited timescale of the project. Joanne commented:

> It felt slightly limiting just having three of us, and we seemed to be from totally different areas. I was First Certificate and Teresa was beginners. So it was interesting but I couldn't relate to it at the time.

It would seem that the potential for successful collaboration was there, but was not always fully exploited. The perceived reluctance to really 'attend', to use Edge's (1992) term, to each other may also have been at least partly due to defensiveness. It is possible that they did not feel sufficiently confident to comment on each other's teaching, and therefore preferred to concentrate on how what was being said might apply to their own situation.

2 To what extent did the project enable the participants to develop confidence in their own capacities to empower themselves and build self-esteem and autonomy?

Even more than I had expected, the teachers, especially Sarah and Claire, frequently expressed self-doubt. As a way of further exploring this area, I asked participants how they felt about asking students to comment on their teaching, something which had been tried at varying degrees of remove. Participants agreed with the idea in principle, regarding it a necessary evil, but there was a reluctance to hand over too much power to the students. Joanne, for example, had tried asking students for feedback but commented that it was not something that she would normally do. She went on to explain:

Sometimes I do feel that the students would say, 'I don't think we ought to do this, this is a waste of time', when I've got very good reasons for doing it ... So to some extent I suppose I feel that if I did I'd open a can of worms.

Sometimes 'feedback' was interpreted in a more limited, and safer, way. Teresa remarked:

I think we should be open to that (student feedback). I do sometimes say to my students, 'Now, how did you find that? Did you enjoy that?' And, for example, the listening I did this morning with them, many of them said, 'Too fast, too fast!'

Teresa was also reluctant to experiment with anything which deviated from her usual classroom practice, feeling that she 'knew' that a suggested approach would or would not work with her students. In the following interchange, Joanne and I are trying to suggest ways in which Teresa might extend the writing skills of her elementary students:

Joanne: There's something I've seen where they're given a poem but it's muddled up, to rearrange it.
Teresa: Oh, in a poem ... they can rearrange sentences, but—
Joanne: Even a story?
Teresa: Oh, I tried that, I did try that and they were very confused. They like doing, they actually like doing things that they find useful I suppose.
Rachael: What do they need to do in terms of writing in their everyday life?
Teresa: Postcards. We've done postcards.
Joanne: What about filling in forms or—
Teresa: Haven't done forms. Letters? We've done informal letters, just short letters. We've done that on the board.
Rachael: Maybe they could write letters to each other? You know, to give them a—
Teresa: I've got a feeling I've done that but they could do that again.
Joanne: Invitations – would you like to come to my party, or something.
Teresa: I think I've covered really all the writing one does with them.

Teachers often preferred to retell successful experiences, in order to gain peer approval, than to discuss problematical areas. While I can certainly see the value of this, I also felt that it was important to stress that doing something inadequately could be even more valuable in terms of the insights it afforded, hoping that, as Elliott (1991:7) also found, 'The more teachers view themselves as action researchers the greater their ability to tolerate losses of self-esteem'. Creating what Underhill (1992) calls 'an atmosphere with understanding, trust and shared commitment (which) can facilitate risk-taking and openness' is possibly not something which could ever be entirely satisfactorily achieved in such a pilot study. Nonetheless, despite the constraints of the pilot study, there were definite signs that the approach could indeed help to develop some teachers' confidence in their own capacities. In the final interview, Claire commented:

It's given, I think it's given me the chance to do something new without feeling that I'm doing it off my own bat, without feeling that I daren't do that. It's forced me into doing something, I've done lots of new things.

3 How successful was the project in providing for a bridge between theory and practice?

Although the teachers were quite happy to discuss the theory behind the teaching of writing they did often feel, as one participant noted, that 'So much of the theory doesn't apply in the classroom.' There was a marked tendency to reject an idea out of hand because it did not fit their own situation rather than examine the principles behind it and decide how it might be adapted. Rather than exploring the reasons for failure and modifying practice accordingly, participants often expressed the opinion that the project would have been more 'successful' if they had been in a more ideal teaching situation. In the final meeting, Sarah suggested:

> For the record, for the future, if anyone wants to try this again, they perhaps try it with a full-time class, who, they're committed, aren't they? Working for something, like the TOEFL group, or EFL Plus.

In general there was a much more positive reaction to what Teresa refers to as 'tips and techniques' than to the process of teacher development itself. Teachers sometimes seemed unwilling or unable to reflect in such a way that they 'transcend the technicalities of teaching and think beyond the need to improve ... instructional techniques' (Bartlett 1990:205). Many of the setbacks or successes experienced by the participants seemed to be due to what I would like to term 'teacher variables': the individual differences in the beliefs teachers hold about teaching and learning and in the ways they go about implementing these beliefs in the classroom.

Knowing-in-action and reflection

It would appear from reading the literature on teacher-initiated research that most if not all teachers were somehow naturally reflective. However, this is not necessarily the case. Wallace refers to two phenomena, described by Schön, which go to make up the experiential knowledge of a teacher: 'knowing-in-action' and 'reflection'. Knowing-in-action is defined by Schön in the following way:

> ... Every competent practitioner ... in his day-to-day practice makes innumerable judgements of quality for which he cannot state criteria and displays skills for which he cannot state the rules and procedure. (Schön 1983 in Wallace 1991:13)

The profession of teaching is no exception. All the participants referred to making such instinctive judgements. Joanne, for example, talked about the way 'you start something with a class and then you slightly adapt it on the way because you have a feeling that it's going to work better that way.' Teachers often need to 'think on their feet'. This ability to make quick instinctive judgements is therefore a vital skill.

However, what would seem to mark a more reflective approach in some of the participants was the way in which these judgements were later assessed, if at all. Teresa tended to measure her success in technical matters, such as timing, and on the instinctive feeling she had about the overall success of the lesson.

> I think to myself, ' I ought to have expanded there,' or 'I rushed them with that,' or 'I've got my timing wrong there.' I don't really analyse that much. I'm just aware, 'That was good, I got that right, they enjoyed it, that's great.'

Similarly, Sarah described the way in which she would 'sort of click it as it goes, "oh, this is working, use this again, oh, this is awful, never going to use this again."'

Sarah and Teresa seemed to rely heavily on knowing-in-action or instinct, rather than reflection. In contrast, both Joanne and Claire seemed to question not only what had been effective but why that might have been so. In some ways it might be possible to draw a correlation between each teacher's propensity for reflection and, for example, their attitude towards keeping the diary – one of the elements of the programme.

Claire was probably the participant who felt that she had gained most from the experience. She was also the only participant, apart from myself, who kept writing her diary regularly and wrote at some length, allowing it to become a conduit for reflection. Joanne also felt positive about the diary: 'it's rather like when you speak to somebody about what's on your mind and you actually realize more as you're actually speaking, than was in there in the first place.' 'I think, in practical terms,' she continued, 'I would be more likely to write, not in a diary but to write something on a lesson plan. But I think now I've done this with you I might be a bit more focused in that now.'

Claire's partner, Sarah, seemed to be not so much analysing herself as keeping a record of more concrete events. She often seemed to use her diary as a place to note problem areas to bring up at meetings, reading aloud from it. Teresa never wrote a word in her diary. She had warned me from the beginning that she did not have much sympathy with the idea:

> I'm very interested to come and share ideas, but the writing is just ... I'm not sure that it would help me ... I don't honestly feel that keeping a diary like this is of any use to me.

A similar division between more and less reflective approaches appears if we compare the participants' planning styles. None of the teachers involved in the project was in the habit of writing detailed lesson plans. Nevertheless, there was still a significant variation in what participants considered was involved in preparing a class. Their approaches could almost be ranged along a continuum. At one end was Teresa, who, said Sarah, 'just sort of thinks, "Oh, I'm going to do this today," and just goes and does it'. Sarah spent more time planning than Teresa, but she also seemed to concentrate largely on the content of the lesson, asking herself, 'What am I going to teach them?' and 'Are they going to be interested in the way I present this?'

Shavelson and Stern suggest that there is 'a mismatch between the demands of classroom instruction and the prescriptive planning model.' This mismatch arises, they argue, because:

> ... teachers must maintain the flow of activity during a lesson or face behavioural management problems. Hence they are faced first and foremost with deciding what activities will engage students during the lesson or put another way, the teacher must decide how to entertain his or her audience while attending to the curriculum. (Shavelson and Stern 1981:477)

Probably every teacher would identify with this to a certain extent but Claire and Joanna did claim to focus their planning primarily on the aims of the lesson:

> If I find I'm sitting there thinking, 'Oh my God, what am I going to do?' ... I literally get a piece of paper and I write down aims, maybe three, and then I think 'OK, well, how are you going to get there?' And it helps me enormously. I do it most of the time.

J. Kennedy, writing about trainee teachers, suggests that, 'it may be that in the early stages of learning to teach, trainees need to concentrate on acquiring a confident grasp of classroom routines and that critical analysis develops at a much later stage.' (J. Kennedy 1993:162.) It is tempting to conclude that the difficulty encountered by some of the participants was due to lack of experience. Certainly it is true that Joanne was the most experienced teacher, but Teresa also had several years' teaching experience. Sarah and Claire had taken an initial training course together two years earlier, and yet showed very different attitudes. It would seem that an individual teacher's approach is probably based on nothing so easily identifiable as the amount of experience gained, but is rather based on what he/she has actually experienced as a teacher and as a learner. Somekh suggests that the routines of teaching 'have been developed in practice ... they have become bound up in our self-image and feelings of professional confidence and security' (Somekh 1993:35). Such routines probably begin to develop long before a teacher ever undergoes training – they may derive them from early learning experiences in childhood at home and school. While all four participants were committed teachers who enjoyed their work, both Teresa and Sarah seemed to feel strongly that they wanted to somehow make a difference. In Teresa's case this was echoed by her attitude towards the students, which tended to be protective:

> They need it controlled, because I set them doing it by themselves and they were in such a flap, and I could see Rubena ... so I said, 'Would you like me to do it with you?' 'Yes, please,' they all said ... and they all copied it and then they knew they'd got it right.

Interestingly, Sarah, who might have been expected to hold quite similar beliefs, remarked, 'I think it's very easy to spoonfeed students and I think it's good for them to take responsibility.' This is of course a reminder that teachers do not fall neatly into two camps. As Elliott notes:

> Dilemmas for insider researchers can arise from a clash of professional values between those which undermine the traditional craft culture and those which underpin an emergent culture of reflective practice. This clash occurs not so much between as within individuals. (Elliott 1991:57)

It is not then a case of reflective and unreflective teachers but of points along a continuum. The important thing is to realize that individuals can interpret and view the same phenomena differently. Rogers and Shoemaker (1971), writing about successful change, refer to the need for compatibility, the extent to which an innovation is perceived as being consistent with the participants' existing values, past experiences and present needs. If it is not felt to be compatible, they suggest it will be undermined or subverted. Clearly the approach which lay behind this project had not proved immediately compatible with some of the values, experiences and needs of at least two of the participants. Wiser, at the end of the project, I realized the importance of this. The project had by no means failed, but it would undoubtedly have been more successful had I known at the beginning what I had discovered by the end.

The results of this research would seem to indicate that some teachers may be more naturally inclined towards reflective practice, while others tend to rely almost entirely upon 'knowing-in-action' or instinct in making their classroom decisions. Experience is seen as important by these teachers mainly because it provides them with a store of 'ideas that are tried and trusted' (Allwright and Bailey 1990). However, as Allwright and Bailey go on to point out, 'In the long run it is not enough to know that ideas do work; we need also to know how and why they work. Until we can throw more light on these issues, successful teaching will remain a mystery.' (ibid:197). If teachers do not understand and cannot make informed choices about their techniques they will remain simply 'highly skilled technicians' (McNiff 1988). For teachers to become experts in their field they need to actively learn from their experience. As Somekh (1993) points out, getting teachers to self-monitor their practice is the first step. This will help them to identify and understand their personal theories – a change in practice may emerge from a change in these theories.

Encouraging a reflective approach

If teachers are, like Teresa, not predisposed towards a critical analysis of practice, what can, or should, be done about it? It is notoriously difficult to attempt to change such deep-rooted beliefs, especially over a short period of time. Calderhead (1987) cites a study by Korthagen which found that in a teacher education course aimed at developing the skills of critical reflection on practice, 'the only students to be influenced appeared to be those who were already disposed towards critically analysing their practice anyway.' As Somekh, previously cited, suggests, such perspectives may form an important part of a teacher's self-image. Pushing teachers to change something so fundamental before they are ready may be counter-productive. A reflective approach may not always be the most suitable approach for a given teacher at a given point in time. Teachers may initially be more concerned with developing effective and efficient teaching routines – they may need to learn to survive before they can begin to reflect on their own practice.

However, with all the potential benefits which appear to accrue to the reflective teacher, it would seem that his/her orientation to development through self-enquiry must still remain an end goal. Rather than trying to force teachers to become more reflective, a thankless and possibly demoralizing task, we might consider ways in which the process can be facilitated.

Kemmis and McTaggart (1988) set out a number of useful suggestions for developing action research projects, to which I would refer the facilitator. However, I would also like to add the following observations, based on experience of this case study and aimed at creating the most favourable climate possible for teachers to develop their reflective capabilities, which I believe may also be generalizable over different contexts.

1   Encourage discussion of and some general agreement on educational goals within the institution as a whole: this may help researchers feel they are working within the institution rather than against it and thus encourage risk-taking.

2   Set up good channels of communication with the management/administration so that potential conflicts may be defused and change made safer.

3   Try to ensure maximum publicity and support from the administration: this may also encourage others to join the research group, leading in turn to less marginalization.

4 Make sure that teachers receive praise and recognition for their work, even if more material benefits are not possible.

5 Maximize participants' sense of ownership. This may be better achieved if:

   a) the research question is not imposed;

   b) the facilitator is not solely responsible for the writing up and publicity of the project.

6 Be patient with teachers who fail to see the benefits of a reflective approach. Publicizing the benefits found by other teachers might help but you may have to accept that there are no benefits for this particular teacher at this stage in their career.

7 Consider ways of helping teachers to develop their reflective abilities. Thornbury (1991), for example, guided teachers in their self-observation tasks by asking them to focus on specific aspects of their practice.

This case study inevitably leaves many questions unanswered, but on a personal level, the process was extremely educative. I began with a rather evangelistic view of the numerous potential benefits of this type of approach and ended, or rather paused, no less convinced of these benefits but better informed about the pitfalls and with some ideas of how I might improve my own practice as a facilitator. From the wider point of view, the study can only be seen as a tiny increment to the knowledge already amassed. Nonetheless, if all those conducting action research continue to investigate its workings in this way, together we may create a fuller picture of what is involved and thus make a difference to the professional situation of participant teachers.

Rachael Roberts' experience extends from English language teaching and teacher training in Brazil, ESP and materials develop-ment in Portugal, to teacher develop-ment work in the UK. She was until recently director of studies at International House in Poland where teacher develop-ment and action research was an important focus of her work.

'This is my portfolio': portfolios in Finnish upper secondary schools

10

Pirjo Pollari

Introduction

T his case study describes a portfolio experiment in the teaching of English as a foreign language in two Finnish upper secondary schools. We wanted to try out portfolios as a new vehicle for teaching, learning and assessment as well as a means for students to negotiate their own syllabuses within the given framework. The topic area of the portfolio course was culture. As student empowerment, learner-centredness and self-directed learning were the key concepts of this experiment, the case study attempts to bring in authentic student experiences by quoting student comments. The comments are unedited and they were written in English by the students themselves.

> My portfolio includes: a poem, a song, a human-analysis, a fairy-tale and a radioplay. They are, I think, a bit unusual, but it's just what I wanted, because I want to be different. I like writing poems and songs. I know these works are myself.

Background

Learner-centredness and self-direction are some of the keywords of contemporary educational discussion in Finland. Learning is currently seen as a process of knowledge and meaning construction based on the learner's own activity and on his or her prior learning. Emphasizing the student's own active role in learning requires a paradigm shift from teacher- or textbook-centred 'transmission of knowledge' to a more student-centred and self-directed approach. It also requires a shift from a basically quite uniform curriculum towards more individual curricula. But how do we do that in practice?

Portfolios have proved to be one of the promising alternatives not only for promoting performance-based assessment but also for learner-centred and self-directed learning. In a school context, a portfolio is a purposeful selection of student work usually collected and selected by the students themselves. The portfolio exhibits the students' efforts, progress and achievements over a period of time. Usually the work also exhibits the students' own choice and interests. The portfolio should include a description of its purpose, goals, and criteria for selection and assessment. Preferably, it contains the

Pollari describes an action research project similar to Roberts' (see previous article) conducted with secondary school teachers of English in Finland. The objective was to implement and evaluate a different approach to learning and teaching – using portfolios. This final case study brings together several themes of the collection. One is the systemic nature of change. The decision to use portfolios goes back to an educational policy in Finland to emphasize more learner-centred education. The policy arises from the perceived need for a thinking, creative workforce able to adapt to changing circum-stances in an uncertain future. Pollari's case study, like many in this collection, shows how new approaches put demands on teachers implementing the change. It also brings a further group of participants into the change process who are crucial to its success: the learners for whom the changes are ultimately designed.

students' own reflection on and evaluation of both the selected work and the process of studying and learning. (See De Fina 1992; Linnakylä 1994; Paulson et al. 1991; Tierney et al. 1991.)

A portfolio experiment in EFL teaching

Three upper secondary school teachers and I as a researcher tried out portfolios in the teaching of English as a foreign language. We planned, carried out and monitored the portfolio experimentation in close co-operation, and it was supported by the Institute for Educational Research of the University of Jyväskylä.

The participating students were all in the second grade of the upper secondary school – aged 17 or 18 – and they had been studying English for almost nine years, 2–3 lessons a week. During the three years of upper secondary school the students have 6–8 thematically based compulsory English courses, each consisting of approximately 35 lessons. We chose one of those courses – the 'culture course' – for the portfolio experiment. This particular course and grade level were chosen mainly for two reasons. Firstly, culture as a topic area was considered to provide an interesting and fruitful basis for students' portfolios, fostering their cultural interests, knowledge and understanding. Secondly, despite considerable individual differences among students, the average proficiency level at that stage, a year before taking their final examinations, is usually quite high. Thus, teaching could more easily focus on the experiential use of the language and more demanding communicative tasks (Clark 1987). Furthermore, the students of that age already have prior knowledge, skills, experiences and interests to build upon and are more mature for an experiment like this.

In addition to studying English and some aspects of culture, one of the central ideas of the portfolio experiment was to promote learner-centred and self-directed learning. (For defining learner-centredness, see eg Tudor 1993). We wanted the students to take greater responsibility for their own work but also to have the freedom and power to make decisions concerning their studying. We also wanted them to learn to set their own goals as well as to assess their work and state their criteria. Furthermore, we thought it important to encourage students to work together and to give feedback to each other. And, most importantly, we wanted our students to feel ownership of their learning and of their abilities to communicate in English. What would be the use of all those years of studying English if they did not feel able and willing to use the language, to communicate in it, and to keep learning more?

The theoretical framework

The ideas mentioned above are mainly based on constructive and socioconstructive views of learning, and by progressivism-oriented curriculum design (Clark 1987). Teaching should be flexible and it should emphasize the learners' capacities. Students should be active agents of their learning, not just passive receivers of information. Learning is a product of the learners' own actions and it is based not only on the learners' prior skills and knowledge but also on their experiences and interests.

Effective, meaningful learning is usually goal-oriented and self-regulated: the students are committed to the goals and, thus, take control over their learning in order to reach those goals. If the learner has a say in defining the goals and deciding the content and methods, learning is usually more relevant to the learner and, thus, more effective (De Corte 1993; Tudor 1993:23–24). Learning is also a situated and social process. Social interaction, negotiation and collaboration as well as authentic learning tasks and contexts are all believed to be characteristics of effective learning (see eg De Corte 1993; Linnakylä 1994; von Wright 1993).

In terms of curriculum design, the new Finnish curricular guidelines promote learner-centred approaches and individualized curricula and study programmes within a given framework. For example, the aims and syllabus of the culture course are defined in the Framework Curriculum for Senior Secondary School (1994:63) as follows:

> Students concentrate on self-directed oral and written work. The subject matter and types of activity are chosen according to students' interests and preferences, and carried out eg as projects. The topics may include eg arts, literature, music, film and theatre.

Students creating their portfolios

All participating groups – altogether about 100 students – had a similar framework which outlined basic requirements for the portfolios. First of all, the pieces of work were expected to be diverse both in their content and form. Both oral and written language – listening, speaking, reading and writing – were to be used either in the product or in the process. Self-assessment as well as giving and getting feedback were also considered important.

First, the students compiled four or five different pieces of work in their working portfolios, and then, at the end of the course, they assessed their work choosing two or three pieces for their final showcase portfolios. The showcase portfolios were then presented and celebrated in the class. Afterwards they were evaluated by the teacher and the students' course grades were based on that. No other tests or exams were taken during this course.

Setting goals and defining criteria

At the very beginning of the course, we discussed the framework and basic requirements of the portfolio course with the students. We also discussed the criteria for assessing student portfolios: the work should exhibit a variety of topics and modes, it should display the student's involvement in and responsibility for his or her work, and use of English should be fairly clear and fluent. Accordingly, grammatical correctness and good vocabulary alone were not the most important criteria for outstanding work.

The students were also given some ideas and background materials to help them set their own goals, choose their topics and plan their work. The development of the actual syllabus for this course thus became a collaborative effort between the students and teachers (Nunan 1988:2). Nevertheless, even though the teacher and other students were there to help, setting one's own goals and planning one's work was not easy for everybody. Students' abilities as well as their willingness to take control of their own learning varied a lot (the words below are the students' own):

> When I started this course my head was really empty, I didn't know what to do.

> I am not very good at English and culture is not my hobby (except for listening the music and watching TV), so at first the whole portfolio looked very difficult. I started to think: 'What to do?' and then I (with my friends' help) found these four subjects.

> All the time, during this course, I was very in this portfolio-working. The theme, arts, was the best possible for me. I was full of different kinds of ideas, so it was easy for me to start working.

The teacher's role was far from easy and simple. Even though the teacher did not have as many classroom lessons as usual, her responsibilities increased. As Tudor, for instance, says (1993:24–9), in a learner-centred approach the teacher performs many different functions, such as helping students develop awareness of learning goals, options and themselves as learners, analysing their needs, transferring responsibility and involving learners in the learning process. All this of course requires many skills in addition to those needed in more traditional modes of teaching – as well as a lot of time and energy (Tudor 1993:29–30).

Self-directed work

> About the schedule: ... err, as you know writing a story can only be done when the moment is right. So I'll be waiting for it. Don't worry, I'm quite sure it will come soon.

During the course of about 35 lessons, the students were expected to attend about 15 lessons. Most of these 15 lessons dealt with the portfolios but there were a couple of grammar lessons and language laboratory lessons as well. Otherwise, the students were free to study when and where they preferred. In order to monitor their work, the students were asked to write notes about their studying in their working logs. Inside and outside the classroom, the students worked both on their own and in pairs or small groups. They were encouraged to come and ask the teacher for help.

Feedback in class conferences

Class conferences were held once a week and there the students were asked to go through each other's work and comment on it in small groups in order to improve it. The teachers also tried to monitor and comment on the students' work while the work was in progress and thus provide immediate feedback as well as support and additional help if needed. In larger groups of 30 or more students, however, this was sometimes quite difficult.

In general, giving feedback was considered very difficult, yet also helpful. To make peer assessment easier, we gave students some basic questions that they might use as a starting point: What was the best or the most interesting thing in this piece of work? Did the piece raise any questions in your mind? Was there something you would like to know more of, or something you did not quite understand? How would you improve the piece? What did you learn from it? However, some students would clearly have benefited from even more guidance and support.

> Every week we had so called 'Class Conference' (CC) meetings where we were supposed to discuss about our portfolios. It didn't work. We did talk about them, but only for five minutes, and after that we just talked about everything else.

> The advices that my friends gave me were very precious.

A wide range of personal pieces of work

The pieces of work the students produced were diverse both in their choices of topic and form. Compared to our suggestions – for instance, a review of a film or a book, or a portrait of an artist and his/her art – the students' portfolios showed a much more varied and comprehensive definition of culture. Book, film or TV reviews were very popular, though. The topics ranged from *Little Women* to J. R. R. Tolkien's whole production; from *The Bold and the Beautiful* to *The Unbearable Lightness of Being*. There were many portraits as well, ranging from Maurice Ravel to Toni Morrison and from Charlie Chaplin to Tom Cruise, to cite a few.

Many students had wanted to express themselves and create something of their own. There were poems, short stories, fairytales, cartoons, and even songs. One student had written a seven-page-long fairytale in rhyming English! Some students had taped their own radio talk shows or radio plays; some had videotaped small plays or films.

Several students had found different source materials for various project papers and essays in English. For example, one student had investigated the Celts and their culture; another student had analysed Kullervo (one of the central characters in the Finnish national epic Kalevala) in Finnish arts and society; and yet another had studied Romanticism in music. In Shakespeare's footsteps, one student presented Stratford-upon-Avon; another discussed the problem of power in Shakespeare's *Julius Caesar*. An old book of American and English poetry had inspired a student to write a booklet about Emily Dickinson and her poetry imitating the 19th century handwriting and illustrations; the Bible had inspired a group of four students to analyse the stylistic differences in two Finnish and English translations of Genesis.

There were also taped discussions or interviews dealing with various aspects of culture. There was, for instance, a poster focusing on a language as part of culture (Five Ways to Love in Greek), another poster presenting the British and the European Union, a brochure about the sights of Guernsey, and a video introducing our local museums. There were essays analysing the students' own hobbies and cultural interests, and papers discussing the effects of violence on television or the role of sports in culture.

Even though a few students defined culture narrowly as only literature or the arts, the diversity of student work really showed that no standard textbook could possibly define and deal with culture as creatively as students themselves could.

The showcase portfolios

Having completed four or five different pieces by the end of the course, the students were asked to choose two or three pieces for their showcase portfolios. The final showcase portfolio also included a prologue introducing the portfolio and the student to the reader.

> I have completed 4 different pieces of work, all having something to do with me and things I like: music, literature, film, poetry ... Finding yourself, as an individual, is important for every one of us. —
> I think that there's something about me captured in this portfolio!

> My works tell a lot of me and my interests. Something about my thoughts and opinions. Probably they show that my English is not perfect, but I've tried my best and I'm developing all the time.

The students were also asked to assess the pieces they had selected. In their criteria for selection the students often emphasized the amount of work, the working process and learning outcomes as well as the personal relevance of the piece.

> Second work I've chosen is my Picasso-work. It's my best work, it's most comprehensive. I've used several sources and did lots of work. It may not seen in this work, but I for example learned hugely new words. I also invested in works looks.

> *Amadeus* has been a truly influential film in my life and I simply wanted to share my passion with others.

> 'The house at pooh corner', a radio-play
> This was a group-work and it was good for me, because my oral skills aren't too good. And it was fun doing it.

> I think my best work was movie review *The three musketeers* because I work it so hard. I think that these work prove that I'm not so lazy and stupid that you thought.

> This work is important for me, because it was my first book, which I have read in English and it takes so much time to clear up it.

Epilogue

The last piece to be included in the final portfolio was an epilogue summing up the student's reflections on his or her learning and on the course in general. Most students – regardless of their prior success in English – considered the course a positive and encouraging, even empowering, experience.

> I'm glad we decided to do something new instead of doing the same things year after another. This was absolutely worth doing.

> I really liked working this way 'cause it gives me the freedom I need to be creative.

> This was a challenging job to do. I spent many hours with my projects. My portfolio looked quite good, I know there's a lot of mistakes but I tried my best.

> For myself, this work gave a lot of self-confidence and I began to feel that I can do at least something in English even though my grades are so poor. (Translated from Finnish by the author.)

Studying have been fun.

This course was very good. Not only because we didn't have lexons. I learnt to take care of those things myself.

Several students said that their writing skills had improved. For example, process writing and feedback were new experiences to some students. Many students mentioned that they had learned to use dictionaries and other sources more readily in their work. Quite a few students said that reading a lot of different, authentic materials had improved their reading skills in English. Some students commented that the skills they had learned during the portfolio course would probably help them in their future studies. For instance, some said that they had learned to accept responsibility for their own work. Many students felt that they were more willing to communicate in English and probably not as afraid of making mistakes as earlier. Feelings of having accomplished something as well as succeeding in their work at their own level motivated students. Some reported that this was the first time in years they had enjoyed studying English at school.

However, some students were more cautious. A number of students said that because they had only had one or two grammar lessons, they had not really learned anything new in English. Some said that they had not had enough practice in speaking English. Some students suggested that portfolios should be optional. Teachers were also cautioned against getting too enthusiastic about portfolios.

I think portfolio is, at the end, good thing. But only when it's given as a special project. If every school subject begins to use it, the idea loses it's charm.

Naturally, there were a few students who did not like the course at all. The course was demanding, and even too demanding for some students. Regardless of the teacher's or other students' assistance, the freedom and responsibility for one's own work caused some problems. Some students never quite realized the diversity of cultural topics.

I didn't like this system at all. Too much work all at once. (Translated from Finnish by the author.)

And what it comes to studying English I would rather do a normal course of English, instead of this hell of games without proper rules.

I didn't like this course in the begin and I don't still like it because I'm not keen in literature.

Teachers assessing the portfolios

The showcase portfolio was assessed by the teacher according to the criteria discussed at the beginning of the course. The evaluation was not always easy. In particular, the teachers found grading the portfolios difficult and even frustrating – how to transform all that work, effort, and creativity into a single grade? However, in addition to the actual grade, the teacher gave a more comprehensive verbal assessment of the portfolio focusing on its strengths but also pointing out possible areas for improvement. We hoped that we could thus make the students see the weaknesses as opportunities for further learning, not as serious flaws or mistakes. And sometimes, I think, we succeeded. Consequently, the verbal assessment, even though it took a lot of the teacher's time, was considered very important. After all, the portfolio is a vehicle for learning as well as for assessment – it is the student's process of learning that is the most important. As a student phrases it:

> The most important thing is that I have succeeded in one way or another and even if I don't get a 10 from this course I'm not disappointed. I have already given myself a 10 from trying and crossing my limits. And the most important thing is that I am satisfied with my works and proud of them!
> (N.B. The grades used in Finland are from 4 to 10, 10 being the best.)

Conclusion

The portfolio experiment taught us all – teachers, students and researchers – that student-centred and self-directed learning is not an easy option. First of all, some students are more willing and also more able to accept responsibility for their own learning. The teacher's role as a facilitator or counsellor of learning requires a lot from the teacher as well. The responsibility should be transferred gradually to the students – and more gradually to some than others. The teacher should support, guide, encourage, and help whenever needed, but refrain whenever it is not needed. Despite our difficulties, and our rather radical student-directed approach, we found the portfolio experiment a positive experience. We discovered new aspects in teaching and learning English but also in one another as persons. The teachers got to know their students better as persons, not only as students of English, and vice versa. We learned in real practice that there are various ways of learning and teaching, and different ways may work better for different people. We all learned to appreciate the potential students have, if only given a proper chance, to be involved in the decision-making in order to find the goals, tasks and methods that suit them best. Most importantly, I am confident that most students gained a lot. At the very least, they had a chance to try their wings in negotiating their own syllabuses and monitoring and assessing their own learning in English.

Pirjo Pollari has worked as both a language teacher and a teacher trainer. She is a researcher at the Teacher Training School at the University of Jyväskylä, Finland.

References and bibliography

Ajzen, I. 1988 *Attitudes, Personality and Behaviour: From Intentions to Actions* (Open University Press)

Alderson, J. C. and Wall, D. 1993 Does washback exist? In *Applied Linguistics* vol. 14 no. 2:115-29 (OUP)

Allwright, D. and Bailey, K. M. 1990 *Focus on the Language Classroom: An Introduction to Classroom Research for Language Teachers* (CUP)

Bailey, K. M. 1990 The use of diary studies in teacher education programmes. In Richards, J. C. and Nunan, D. (eds.) 1990

Bartlett, L. 1990 Teacher development through reflective teaching. In Richards, J. C. and Nunan, D. (eds.) 1990

Bolam, R. 1976 *New Patterns of Teacher Education and Tasks: Teachers as Innovators* (OECD, Paris)

Breen, M., Candlin, C., Dam, L. and Gabrielsen, G. 1989 The evolution of a teacher training programme. In Johnson, R. K. (ed.) 1989 *The Second Language Curriculum* (CUP)

Brumfit, C., Phillips, M. and Skehan, P. (eds.) 1985 Computers in English Language Teaching: A view from the classroom. In *British Council Occasional Papers* no. 122 (British Council/ Pergamon)

Buchanan, D. and Boddy, D. 1992 *The Expertise of the Change Agent* (Prentice Hall)

Butler-Wall, B. 1979 Diary Studies. In Arafa, E., Brown, C., Butler-Wall, B. and Early, M. *Classroom Observation and Analysis* (unpublished manuscript, Applied Linguistics PhD program, University of California, Los Angeles)

Calderhead, J. (ed.) 1987 *Exploring Teachers' Thinking* (Cassell)

Carless, D. R. and Lee, I. K. B. 1994 Attitude changes on an INSET course for primary teachers. In *Hong Kong Institute of Language in Education Journal* vol. 11:56-75

Carter, R. and McCarthy, M. 1988 *Vocabulary and Language Teaching* (Longman)

Charles, M. 1990 Responding to problems in written English using a student self-monitoring technique. In *ELT Journal* vol. 44. no. 4 (OUP)

Chin, R. and Benne, K. D. 1976 General strategies for effecting changes in human systems. In Bennis, W. G., Benne, K. D., Chin, R. and Corey, K. D. (eds.) 1976 *The Planning of Change* (Holt, Rinehart and Winston, New York)

Clark, J. L. 1987 *Curriculum Renewal in School Foreign Language Learning* (OUP)

Clark, J. L. 1988 Curriculum development across languages and across sectors of education. In Bickley, V. (ed.) 1988 *Languages in Education in a Bi-Lingual or Multi-Lingual Setting* (Hong Kong Education Department)

Clark, J. L., Scarino, A. and Brownell, J. A. 1994 *Improving the Quality of Learning: A Framework for Target-Oriented Curriculum Renewal in Hong Kong* (Hong Kong Institute of Language in Education)

Cleverley, J. 1985 *The Schooling of China* (Allen and Unwin)

De Corte, E. 1993 *Learning Theory and Instructional Science.* Paper presented at St. Gallen, Switzerland, 5-6 March 1993

De Fina, A. 1992 *Portfolio Assessment: Getting Started* (Scholastic Professional Books, New York)

Delano, L., Riley, L. and Crookes, G. 1994 The meaning of innovation for ESL teachers. In *System* vol. 22 no. 4 (Pergamon)

Dunkel, P. (ed.) 1991 *Computer-Assisted Language Learning and Testing: Research Issues and Practice* (Newbury House)

Edge, J. 1992 *Cooperative Development* (Longman)

Edge, J. and Richards, K. (eds.) 1993 *Teachers Develop Teachers Research* (Heinemann)

Education Department 1990 *Education Commission Report no. 4* (Hong Kong Education Department)

Education Department 1992a *General Introduction to Targets and Target-related Assessment* (Hong Kong Education Department)

Education Department 1992b *Targets and Target-related Assessment: An Overview* (Hong Kong Education Department)

Edwards, C. 1996 Learning to learn how to teach. In Willis, J. and D. *Challenge and Change in Language Teaching* (Heinemann)

Elliott, J. 1991 *Action Research for Educational Change* (Open University Press)

Everard, K. B. and Morris, G. 1985 *Effective School Management* (Paul Chapman, London)

Framework Curriculum for Senior Secondary School 1994 (National Board of Education/Painatuskeskus, Helsinki)

Fullan, M. 1991 *The New Meaning of Educational Change* (Cassell)

Gilpin, A. 1997 Cascade training. In McGrath, I. (ed.) 1997:185-94

Gross, N., Giacquinta, J. B. and Bernstein, M. 1971 *Implementing organizational innovations: a sociological analysis of planned educational change* (Harper Row, New York)

Haigh, G. 1992 A concept of quality. In *Times Educational Supplement* 12/6/92:19

Hall, A. and Baumgartner, P. (eds.) 1991 *Language Learning with Computers* (WISL, Klagenfurt, Austria)

Handy, C. 1991 *Gods of Management* (Business Books, London)

Handy, C. and Aitken, R. 1986 *Understanding Schools As Organisations* (Penguin)

Hargreaves, D. 1994 *Changing teachers, changing times* (Cassell)

Havelock, R. and Huberman, M. 1983 *Solving Educational Problems* (UNESCO, Paris)

Havelock, R. G. 1971 The utilization of educational research and development. In *British Journal of Educational Technology* vol. 2 no. 2:84-97

Hedge, T. 1988 *Writing* (OUP)

Higgins, J. 1988 *Language, Learners and Computers* (Longman)

Higgins, J. and Johns, T. 1984 *Computers in Language Learning* (Collins)

Hirvela, A. and Law, E. 1991 A survey of local English teachers' attitudes towards English and ELT. In *Hong Kong Institute of Language in Education Journal* vol. 8:25-38

Hofstede, G. 1991 *Cultures and Organizations* (McGraw Hill)

Holliday, A. 1992 Tissue rejection and informal orders in ELT projects: collecting the right information. In *Applied Linguistics* vol. 13 no. 4:403-24 (OUP)

Holmes, B. 1985 Policy formulation, adoption and implementation in democratic society. In Lauglo, J. and McLean, M. (eds.) 1985

Hong Kong Standard 25/4/1993 *New scheme delay welcomed*

Hughes, M., Ribbins, P. and Thomas, H. (eds.) 1985 *Managing Education: The System and the Institution* (Holt, Rinehart and Winston, New York)

Hurst, P. 1983 Implementing educational change - a critical review of the literature. In *EDC Occasional Papers* no. 5 (University of London Institute of Education)

Hurst, P. 1985 Decentralisation: panacea or red herring? In Lauglo, J. and McLean, M. (eds.) 1985

Hutchinson, T. 1991 The Management of Change. In *IATEFL Newsletter* no. 111 (IATEFL)

Johns, T. and King, P. (eds.) 1991 Classroom concordancing. In *ELR Journal* vol. 4 (University of Birmingham)

Jones, C. and Fortescue, S. 1987 *Using Computers in the Language Classroom* (Longman)

Kadepurkar, H. 1997 Towards evaluation of teacher training. In McGrath, I. (ed.) 1997:195-203

Kemmis, S., Atkin, R. and Wright, E. 1997 How do students learn? (Occasional Paper no. 5, CARE, University of East Anglia)

Kemmis, S. and McTaggart, R. 1988 *The Action Research Planner* (Deakin University Press, Victoria)

Kennedy, C. 1987 Innovating for a change: teacher development and innovation. In *ELT Journal* vol. 41 no. 3:163-71 (OUP)

Kennedy, C. 1988 Evaluation of ELT projects. In *Applied Linguistics* vol. 9 no. 4:329-42 (OUP)

Kennedy, C. 1989 *Language Planning and English Language Teaching* (Prentice Hall)

Kennedy, C. 1996 Teachers as agents of change. In O'Dwyer (ed.) *Quality management of change* (University of Bilkent, Ankara, Turkey)

Kennedy, C. 1997 Training teachers as change agents. In McGrath, I. (ed.) 1997

Kennedy, C. and Kennedy, J. 1996 Teacher attitudes and change implementation. In *System* vol. 24 no. 3:351-60

Kennedy, J. and Kennedy, C. (forthcoming) Levels, linkages and networks in cross-cultural innovation. In *System* (Pergamon)

Kennedy, J. 1993 Meeting the needs of teacher trainees on teaching practice. In *ELT Journal* vol. 47. no. 2 (OUP)

Kuhn, T. 1970 *The Structure of Scientific Revolutions* (University of Chicago Press)

Last, R. 1984 *Language Teaching and the Microcomputer* (Blackwell)

Lauglo, J. and McLean, M. (eds.) 1985 *The Control of Education* (Heinemann)

Leech, G. and Candlin, C. (eds.) 1986 *Computers in English Language Teaching and Research* (Longman)

Lieberman, A. and Miller, L. (eds.) 1991 *Staff Development for Education in the 90s* (Teachers' College Press)

Lin, J. 1993 *Education in Post-Mao China* (Praeger Publishers, Westport, CT)

Linnakylä, P. 1994 *Mika ihmeen portfolio? Arvioinnin ja oppimisen liitto* (*What portfolio? A union of assessment and learning*). In Linnakylä, P., Pollari, P. and Takala, S. (eds.) *Portfolio oppimisen ja arvioinnin tukena* (*Portfolios as a vehicle for assessment and learning*) (Institute for Educational Research, University of Jyväskylä)

Llewellyn, J. 1982 *A Perspective on Education in Hong Kong: Report by a Visiting Panel* (Hong Kong Government Printer)

Loucks-Horsley, S. and Stiegelbauer, S. 1991 Using Knowledge of Change to Guide Staff Development. In Lieberman, A. and Miller, L. (eds.) 1991

MacDonald, B. 1991 From Innovation to Reform - A Framework for Analysing Change. Introduction in Rudduck, J. (ed.) 1990

Markee, N. 1997 *Managing Curriculum Innovation* (CUP)

McDonough, J. 1994 A teacher looks at teacher diaries. In *ELT Journal* vol. 48 no. 1 (OUP)

McGrath, I. (ed.) 1997 *Learning to Train* (Prentice Hall)

McLaughlin, W. M. 1991 Enabling Professional Development. In Lieberman, A. and Miller, L. (eds.) 1991

McLean, M. and Lauglo, J. 1985 Rationales for decentralization and a perspective from organization theory. In Lauglo, J. and McLean, M. (eds.) 1985

McNiff, J. 1988 *Action research: principles and practice* (Macmillan)

Ministry of Education, Malaysia 1985 *Report of the Cabinet Committee* (Berita Publishing, Kuala Lumpur)

Ministry of Education, Malaysia 1990 *Syllabus specifications for Form 4* (Dewan Bahasa and Pustaka, Kuala Lumpur)

Morris, P. 1985 Teachers' perceptions of the barriers to the implementation of a pedagogic innovation: a South East Asian case study. In *International Review of Education* vol. 31:3-17

Morris, P. 1988 Teachers' attitudes towards a curriculum innovation: an East Asian study. In *Research in Education* vol. 40:75-87

Morris, P. 1990 Bureaucracy, Professionalisation and School-Centred Innovation Strategies. In *International Review of Education* vol. 36:21-41

Nicholls, A. 1983 *Managing Educational Innovations* (Allen and Unwin)

Nicholls, L. 1992 Computers as a stimulus for talk: the nature of talk generated by pairs of students using Storyboard. In *ON-CALL* vol. 9 no. 2:19-29 (University of Queensland, Australia)

Nunan, D. 1988 *The Learner-centred Curriculum* (CUP)

Nunan, D. 1989 *Understanding Language Classrooms* (Prentice Hall)

Nunan, D. 1990 Action research in the language classroom. In Richards, J. C. and Nunan, D. (eds.) 1990

Papert, S. 1987 Computer criticism vs. technocratic thinking. In *Educational Research* 17:22-30 (NFER, Routledge)

Paulson, F. L., Paulson, R. P. and Meyer, C.A. 1991 What makes a portfolio a portfolio? In *Educational Leadership* vol. 48 no. 5:60-3 (ASCD, Alexandria, VA)

Pennington, M. (ed.) 1989 *Teaching Languages with Computers: The State of the Art* (Athelstan)

Pennington, M. 1996 *The Power of CALL* (Athelstan)

Pennington, M. and Stevens, V. (eds.) 1992 *Computers in Applied Linguistics: an International Perspective* (Multilingual Matters)

Perkins, D. N. 1985 The fingertip effect: how information-processing technology shapes thinking. In *Educational Research* 14:11-16 (NFER, Routledge)

Phillips, M. 1985 Logical possibilities and classroom scenarios for the development of CALL. In Brumfit, C., Phillips, M. and Skehan, P. (eds.) 1985

Renouf, A. 1987 Moving on. In Sinclair (ed.) 1987

Richards, J. and Nunan, D. (eds.) 1990 *Second Language Teacher Education* (CUP)

Rinvolucri, M. 1981 Resistance to change on in-service teacher training courses. In *Recherches et Echanges* vol. 6 no. 1

Rogers, E. and Shoemaker, F. 1971 *Communication of Innovations: A Cross Cultural Approach* (The Free Press, New York)

Rogers, E. M. 1983 *Diffusion of Innovations* (Collier-MacMillan, New York)

Rudduck, J. 1990 *Innovation and Change* (McGraw Hill)

Schön, D. A. 1983 *The Reflective Practitioner: How Professionals Think in Action* (Arena, Aldershot)

Shavelson, R. and Stern, P. 1981 Research on teachers' pedagogical thoughts, judgements, decisions and behaviour. In *Review of Educational Research* vol. 51 no. 4:455-98 (AERA, Washington DC)

Sinclair, J. McH. (ed.) 1987 *Looking Up* (Collins)

Sinclair, J. McH. 1991 *Corpus, Concordance, Collocation* (OUP)

Sinclair, J. McH. and Renouf, A. 1988 The Lexical Syllabus. In Carter, R. and McCarthy, M. 1988

Slater, D. 1985 The management of change: the theory and the practice. In Hughes, M., Ribbins, P. and Thomas, H. (eds.) 1985

Somekh, B. 1993 Quality in educational research – the contribution of class-room teachers. In Edge, J. and Richards, K. (eds.) 1993

South China Morning Post 24/4/1993 *Teaching programme put on hold*

Thornbury, S. 1991 Watching the whites of their eyes: the use of teaching prac-tice logs. In *ELT Journal* vol. 43 no. 4 (OUP)

Tierney, R., Carter, M. and Desai, L. 1991 *Portfolio Assessment in the Reading–Writing Classroom* (Christopher-Gordon Publishers, Inc., Norwood, MA)

Times Educational Supplement (unattributed article) 24/5/91:4-6 *Review of the White Paper*

Toffler, A. 1992 *Power Shift* (Bantam Press)

Tudor, I. 1993 Teacher roles in the learner-centred classroom. In *ELT Journal* vol. 47 no. 1:22-31 (OUP)

Underhill, A. 1992 The role of groups in developing teacher self-awareness. In *ELT Journal* vol. 46 no. 1 (OUP)

Underwood, J. H. 1984 *Linguistics, Computers and the Language Teacher: a Communicative Approach* (Newbury House)

Von Wright, J. 1993 *Oppimiskäsitysten historiaa ja pedagogisia seurauksia* (*The history of the concepts of learning and their pedagogical implications* (National Board of Education/Painatuskeskus, Helsinki)

Wallace, M. 1991 *Training Foreign Language Teachers: a reflective approach* (CUP)

Wallace, M. 1998 *Action Research* (CUP)

White, R. 1988 *The ELT Curriculum: Design, Innovation and Management* (Blackwell)

White, R., Martin, M., Stimson, M. and Hodge, R. 1991 *Management in English Language Teaching* (CUP)

Willis, D. 1990 *The Lexical Syllabus* (Collins)

Woodward, T. 1991 *Models and Metaphors in Language Teacher Training* (CUP)

Young, R. and Lee, S. 1985 EFL cur-riculum innovation and teachers' attitudes. In Larson, P., Judd, E. L. and Messerschmitt, D. S. (eds.) *On TESOL '84: A Brave New World for TESOL* (TESOL, Alexandria, VA)

Young, R. and Lee, S. 1987 EFL curriculum innovation and teachers' attitudes. In Lord, R. and Cheng, H. N. L. (eds.) 1987 *Language Education in Hong Kong* (Chinese University Press, Hong Kong)

Index